with thee, and be thy guide,
ıeed to go by thy side.

EVERYMAN'S LIBRARY
EDITED BY ERNEST RHYS

POETRY & THE DRAMA

THE GOLDEN BOOK OF S. T. COLERIDGE
INTRODUCTION BY STOPFORD A. BROOKE

SAMUEL TAYLOR COLERIDGE, born in 1772 and educated at Christ's Hospital and Cambridge. Joined Wordsworth in issuing *Lyrical Ballads* in 1798 and went to live in the Lake District. Visited Malta, Rome, and Germany. Died in 1834. age 36

young man

master of poetic harmony

44
118

56
34

THE GOLDEN BOOK
CF COLERIDGE

PR 4472
F45

LONDON: J. M. DENT & SONS LTD.
NEW YORK: E. P. DUTTON & CO. INC.

PREFACE

I HAD originally intended to place in this book of
Selections only the very best poems of Coleridge,
those which make his position among English
poets unique. The Imagination puts on in them
a garment different from that worn by her in the
heart of other poets, many coloured, and of strange
device. But these are so very few that the book,
I was warned, would be too small, and moreover
would not represent enough of the mind of Coleridge. A good number also of poems would be
left out which are delightful to read, and though
of the second class, of high excellence in that class.
I have therefore included these poems, and a few
more not so good, which have not only a strong
personal interest, but also illustrate his desultory
and wandering verse—drifting phantasies of song,
like *The Picture*; original in form, unshaped by
art, yet shaped enough to make us regret that he

did not pursue the new veins he opened, and mould their metal into a finished sculpture. However, the best poems have, as it were of their own accord, got together in this book.

I have also, as I think lawful in *Selections*, left out, in a few poems, stanzas and lines which seemed to me to injure the impression of the whole. Anyone can read the omissions in the many complete editions of Coleridge, and can agree or disagree with my boldness, as they please. I have done this in the case of *Reflections on leaving a place of Retirement : Fears in Solitude : Lines composed in a Concert Room : A Christmas Carol : The Snow-Drop :* and *A Day Dream.* The rest of the poems are printed as they stand.

I have to express my thanks to Messrs Macmillan, to Mr E. Coleridge, and to Mr Dykes Campbell, for permission to insert a few poems which, until Mr Dykes Campbell's late Edition of Coleridge, had remained in MS. That Edition, which every one who cares for Coleridge ought to consult, has notes attached to it, so careful and so complete, that they do away with any necessity of notes of mine. All possible information has been given in them, not only with regard to the poems themselves, but with regard to all that has been written about them by Lamb, by Wordsworth and by others. Every lover of Coleridge is grateful to Mr Dykes Campbell for this Edition and for the admirable *Life* which accompanies it.

STOPFORD A. BROOKE.

THE FOLLOWING IS A LIST OF COLERIDGE'S WORKS

Greek Prize Ode on the Slave Trade, Cambridge, 1792. Monody on the Death of Chatterton (First draft), 1794. The Fall of Robespierre, An Historic Drama (Coleridge & Southey), 1794. Contributions to "The Cambridge Intelligencer" and "The Morning Chronicle," 1794-1795. The Watchman, 1796. Poems on Various Subjects, 1796. The Vision of the Maid of Orleans (Southey's "Joan of Arc"), republished as "The Destiny of Nations," 1796. Ode on the Departing Year, 1796. Contributions to "The Monthly Magazine," 1796-1797. Fears in Solitude; France, An Ode; Frost at Midnight, 1798. Lyrical Ballads, 1798 (containing "The Ancient Mariner" and other poems). Contributions to "The Morning Post," 1798-1802. Poems in Annual Anthology, 1799-1800. Wallenstein (from the German of Schiller), 1800. Contributions in Prose and Verse to "The Courier," 1807-1811. The Friend, June 1, 1809—March 15, 1810. Contributions to Southey's "Omniana," 1812. Remorse, 1813 (Remodelled from "Osorio" written in 1797, published 1873). Essays on the Fine Arts (Felix Farley's Bristol Journal, 1814). Christabel; Kubla Khan; Pains of Sleep, 1816 (first and second parts of Christabel written 1797 and 1800). The Statesman's Manual, or the Bible the best Guide to Political Skill and Foresight, 1816. Sibylline Leaves, 1817. Zapolya, A Christmas Tale, 1817. Biographia Literaria, 1817. On Method (Essay forming the General Introduction to "Encyclopædia Metropolitana," 1817-1818). Contributions to "Blackwood's Magazine," 1819-1822. Aids to Reflection, 1825. On the Constitution of the Church and State, 1830. A Moral and Political Lecture, 1795. Conciones ad Populam; or, Addresses to the People, 1795. The Plot Discovered: an Address to the People, 1795. First Collected Edition of Poems and Dramas, 1828.

POSTHUMOUS WORKS

Specimens of his Table Talk, edited by H. N. Coleridge, 1835. Letters, Conversations, and Recollections of Samuel Taylor Coleridge, edited by T. Allsop, 1836, '58, '64. Literary Remains, edited by H. N. Coleridge, 1836-1839. Confessions of an Inquiring Spirit, edited by H. N. Coleridge, 1840. Hints towards the Formation of a more Comprehensive Theory of Life, edited by S. B. Watson, 1848. Notes and Lectures upon Shakespeare and some of the Old Dramatists, edited by Sara Coleridge, 1849. Essays on his own Times, edited by S. Coleridge, 3 vols., 1850. Notes upon English Divines, edited by Derwent Coleridge, 1853. Notes, Theological, Political, and Miscellaneous, edited by D. Coleridge, 1853. Lectures on Shakespeare, from Notes by J. P. Collier, 1856. Poetical and Dramatic Works, founded on the Author's latest edition of 1834, edited by R. H. Shepherd, 4 vols., London and Boston, 1877-1881. Complete Works, edited by Professor Shedd, 1884. Miscellanies, Aesthetic and Literary, edited by T. Ashe, 1885. The Poetical Works of Samuel Taylor Coleridge, edited by James Dykes Campbell, 1893. Letters of Samuel Taylor Coleridge, 1785-1834, edited by E. H. Coleridge, 2 vols., 1895.

CONTENTS

I.—MEDITATIVE POEMS.

II.—ODES AND HYMNS.

III.—THE ANCIENT MARINER, AND OTHER POEMS.

IV.—LOVE POEMS.

INTRODUCTION.

SAMUEL TAYLOR COLERIDGE was born in 1772, and died in 1834. His early poems were published in 1796, and the earliest of them was written about ten years before, when he was fourteen years of age The *Ode on the Departing Year* appeared in 1796. In the next two years he wrote *The Ancient Mariner, Kubla Khan*, the first part of *Christabel, The Ode to France*, and a few other poems of singular beauty. His translation of *Wallenstein* was published in 1800, and there are passages in it in which the golden fire of 1797 flames and glows. He said that he hated this translating work; but when he tried original drama, he did not succeed. *Osorio*, first written in 1797, and recast afterwards as *Remorse*, is only patched with poetry. *The Ancient Mariner* was the first of *The Lyrical Ballads* in 1798; and the second part of *Christabel* was written in 1800-1801. Sixteen years afterwards, in the preface to the publication of *Christabel* (1816) he writes: " Since the latter date (that is, since 1800-1) my poetic powers have been, till very lately, in a state of suspended animation. But as, in my very first conception of the tale, I had the whole present to my mind, with the wholeness, no less than the liveliness of a vision, I trust that I shall be able to embody in verse the three parts yet to come in the course of the present year." It was a vain hope. But it cannot be said that his poetic power during all these years was as half-dead as he seemed to think. The noble ode *Dejection*, written in 1802, declares the glory of his handiwork. In 1807 the melancholy splendour of the poem *To a Gentleman, William Wordsworth*, shines clear; and the lovely songs in *Zapolya*, in which he recaptured " the first fine careless rapture," seem to have been written as late as 1815. There are other fine poems, but it is plain that after 1802, his hand struck his lyre less and less frequently, and with a feebler and feebler touch. Some beautiful things were composed, at long intervals, after 1819, and, as in *Youth and Age*, with a perfect sweetness and sadness. But what he had been of old he was no more.

We may then say that his actual poetic life is included within five years, and of these, two only—1797-98—were productive of his best work. He was then twenty-five years old. About the age of thirty he was lost to art in philosophic theology, in political and critical metaphysics. Literature claims him thus in Prose, and the prose-work has its distinct place in the progress of English wisdom and sentiment. It is full of kindling thought, and of thought gorgeously enriched by emotion; but some of us would willingly give away the greater part of it for one more poem as enchanting as *The Ancient Mariner*.

The cause of this decline and fall was opium-eating, and more than enough has been said about it from the moral point of view. The mass of right and gentle-thinking folk are thoroughly sick of the Pharisaic habit in which so many writers indulge, of making the great poets as well as other men of genius the moral object-lessons of mankind, or of using their errors, especially in matters relating to women, as the ground for endless discussions in biographies, reviews, sermons, and the daily press. These discussions minister to the ugliest of all the cravings of Society. It is a loathsome office, and the purveyors are more to blame than the consumers. The faults of men who have glorified their country and the human race are used to gratify the lowest desires of mankind; and this is done, with special vileness, in the name of morality. But there is no morality without love, and none which is not founded on the forgiveness of sins. These writers, on the contrary, continue the remembrance of sins from year to year, establish the pagan conception of retribution, and make punishment eternal. Those whom God and Man have long since forgiven they haul up again for judgment. It is the worst of immoralities.

The long discussion about Shelley and his wife and Mary Godwin is intolerable, and as uninteresting, except to those whose nectar is scandal and whose ambrosia is gossip. And how wicked it has been! It has turned men's eyes away from the permanent and noble in him to the transient and the commonplace. The reverence due to his work has been

lowered, and this is an injury to mankind. Even
Matthew Arnold was carried away into a ludicrous
attempt to make Shelley vulgar. He might as well
have tried to vulgarise the star Arcturus. A host of
grubbing persons spent their time and our patience in
penetrating into the remotest recesses of the business
of Harriet Westbrook, as if it were a lovely landscape. All that needed telling of the story could have
been told in a page, and ten lines more would have
sufficed to say that it was a most unhappy affair;
that Shelley thought that he was right at the time;
that the world thought he was wrong; that he was
punished by the world, and that he took his punishment quietly. The rest belongs to silence.

The last attack on Byron was even more revolting.
Only evil was done by it; to dwell on evil multiplies
evil. When time has veiled, like charity, what is
wrong or ugly, we might be left alone to love what a
poet has written with truth and passion. When those
who preach about Byron can write as well as he
wrote, they may perhaps venture to speak of his sins,
but they are not likely to fulfil that condition. And
the thing to say to those who have some right to
speak, is—" Let him who is without sin among you
first cast a stone."

As to Coleridge, the moralizers have been even
more offensive about him than about Byron or
Shelley. The life of every famous man is a lesson to
the world, but the lesson is spoilt when it is made, as
Thackeray did in his distressing fashion, the text of
moral blame. Of course, there should be no conceal-

ment of the facts of a great man's life. But these
should be stated, when they are bad, without note
or comment. Then every man can apply their lesson
to himself, and with a great deal more force than
when they are loaded with preachments, and
lectured on as if they were anatomical prepara-
tions. The sins of the dead past should not be dis-
cussed, but forgotten. But the good, the things that
are well done, what is beautiful and loving, should
be brought into clearer and clearer light. This is
the practical matter—that is, the matter which helps
and kindles mankind towards the things that are
worthy of worship—which is the proper definition
of the practical. Moreover, evil can never be clearly
understood by us; we are wholly incompetent to
moralise on the ill-doings of men. But good can
always be understood, and its praise is possible on
the lips of a child.

In the case of the poets, we may well be content,
if we are hungry for moral lessons, with what they
say about themselves. They are, for the most part,
exceedingly personal, their own best commentary,
and being self-sensitive to a great degree, are likely
to censure themselves too much for justice. We
should subtract rather than add to the blame they
bestow on themselves. Coleridge is, for example, the
severest critic of his own faults, yet, when we have
read all that he says, nothing remains in our hearts
but pity, not the pity which is akin to self-congratu-
lation or contempt, but that which is akin to love.
For surely few men have ever loved mankind more

than this large-hearted creature of the sunny mist.
And inasmuch as he loved much, his faults are forgiven. Nay more, he has done more good to mankind,
with all his failings, than those unloving persons,
with all their righteousness, who are fond of hissing
or roaring at their fellows, and who have a special
bitterness against the gentle people whose lovingness
silently rebukes them. It is hard to understand why
Carlyle, in whom there was a turbulent spring of
loving-kindness, should have been so brutal to two
of the gentlest of human beings, to Lamb and to
Coleridge. I suppose his own cleverness in slashing
intoxicated him; but that is a worse intoxication
than one caused by opium or by alcohol. Moreover,
he had no sense of beauty, and was wholly incapable
of feeling Poetry. Had he known himself, he ought
never to have written a line about the poets. When
he attempted to write about Lamb or Coleridge, he
became more and more untrue to the men the more
blazingly clever he was. It may be said of him, in
excuse—though there is no excuse for his odious
snarling at Lamb—that he saw Coleridge when he
was old, when the poet was almost worn out of him.
Nevertheless, a just man, or a man who had any
sense of beauty, and who was the master and not the
servant of his own word-painting, would have remembered the young poet in the old mystic, and
thought of what had been. Then reverence and pity
would have stolen into the sketch he made. However, Carlyle was terribly punished. The Gods are
just. They left Carlyle to prefer the poems of Schiller

to those of Coleridge, and Jean Paul Richter to
Charles Lamb.

There is one thing more to say in this connection,
and it may be found in Mr Dykes Campbell's Life of
Coleridge. It is a pleasure to read a biography of
Coleridge which, while it conceals nothing, neither
bemoans the poet as a wreck, nor uses his weakness
to display the moral patronage of a sermon. Mr
Campbell loves his subject, and the result is that
we have a truer picture of Coleridge than we ever
had before. And it is quite plain that if Coleridge
had been a victim of opium, he ended by almost a
victory over his failing. From the time that he
voluntarily placed himself under medical care, he
lived in constant self-command. The strife to overcome the craving for opium is an awful strife, and
few there be that find power to live after it with
intellectual and spiritual excellence. Coleridge did
both for many years, and if the moralists must
handle him, it is on this that they should dwell, for
in this is the true lesson to mankind.

At the beginning, however, of this Essay we need
not look at the old man, worn with many ills, but at
the eloquent and fiery youth, radiant with joy, who,
with the unconscious prophecy of genius, dreamt,
like Joseph, that the sun and the moon and the
eleven stars made obeisance to him. The preface to
the *Juvenile Poems* opens a part of his mind to us
when he was twenty-four years old. The defence of
the necessary egotism of a poet is there made with
an agreeable subtlety, with a winding in and out of

his thinking among the outskirts of his subject, and
then with a sudden emotional dash into its centre
which is characteristic of all Coleridge's writing to
the end of his life. His matter changed, but his
manner is always the same. The languid meditative-
ness of his character, combined with hours of ardent
delight in all things; his child-like pity for himself;
the imaginative dreaminess, which he had not enough
physical animation to continuously meet in battle,
to which we owe part of his special charm, and which
was never ungraceful, for it was mixed with so much
love; the self-thinking, in which he was more pleased
with the thinking than with the self—are already
contained in this preface, and are still more vividly
present in the poems that follow it. Then he reveals
himself also in his haughty acceptance of the public
blame at two points, in his haughtier promise to
amend, save when to reduce glitter of diction would
in his artist opinion spoil the impression of the whole;
in his scornful rejection of the public blame for his
obscurity, and in his quiet assertion that he was not
obscure but that the public were deficient in intelli-
gence. "Intelligibilia, non intellectum adfero."
These things are the very man, and he preserved
to the close this steady faith in the artist's immeasurable distance from his critics.

> "No! laugh, and say aloud in tones of glee,
>   'I hate the quacking tribe, and they hate me.'"

But while Coleridge allows that his *Juvenile Poems*
are self-descriptive, he also claims that for this very

reason they help mankind. They were written, he says, to relieve his own soul of the burden of emotion and thought; and the good of them would be found by those, who, feeling as he felt, could not shape their feeling into thought or words. He did this work for them, and it is an artist's work. I hope, however, that not many persons, save in self-dramatising fancy, as I think it was now with him,* are often as sad as Coleridge is in these poems. It seems to be " high fantastical " when he declares that his pilgrimage through life has been sorrowful and solitary, or recalls an earlier time when he lived in the sunrise of hope, and contrasts it with the storm-tossed life of twenty-two!

> " Life's current then ran sparkling to the noon,
>   Or silvery stole beneath the pensive moon;
>   Ah! now it works rude brakes and thorns among,
>   Or o'er the rough rock bursts and foams along."

Yet it may be that this was true for the moment. He was even in youth a " thought-bewildered man." He was always conscious of power; but also conscious of want of will to use his power; and these two consciousnesses strove within him, and weakened him into despair. Only at high moments he flashed beyond the painful struggle into the upper world of creation.

> " To me hath Heaven with bounteous hand assigned
>   Energic Reason and a shaping mind,
>   The daring ken of Truth, the Patriot's part,
>   And Pity's sigh that breathes the gentle heart.

---

* His disappointment in love was perhaps the main cause of all this youthful sorrow.

> Sloth-jaundiced all! and from my graspless hand
> Drop Friendship's precious pearls, like hour-glass sand.
> I weep, yet stoop not! the faint anguish flows
> A dreamy pang in Morning's feverish doze."

Tired sentinel over himself, who never calls the soldiers of the soul to arms!

Beyond this revelation of himself there are many other matters of interest in these early poems. First, their poetry belongs to that time of transition in England which intervened between the work of Gray or of Collins, and the outburst of a new flood of song in *The Lyrical Ballads*. Wordsworth's *Evening Walk* belongs to that time, but is more coloured with the dawn of the future than with the sunset of the past poetry. Wordsworth was original from the beginning. But the earlier poems of Coleridge are full of the transition. They sometimes imitate Gray, and sometimes Collins; but they do not even touch the excellences of either poet. The impersonations of the passions, the virtues and vices in which Gray indulged, his reflective morality, his mannerisms of the scholar, and his hermit-like generalisations of human life— excellent in form, exceedingly limited in range—are carried to their extremes by Coleridge, and made absurd. The past poetry existed in the imitation; the new life of the future poetry appeared in the youthful exaggeration of the imitation. The coming spirit worked in Coleridge like puffing leaven, and sonorous and six-footed words and big-bellied images and metaphors separated Coleridge from Gray, still more from his more poetic brother, neither of whom could have read a line of *The Religious Musings* without a shudder.

The reticent grace of Collins, his literary gentleness, his subdued and sunset note, the dusky veil he drew over his expression—even in a description like that of joy in the *Ode to the Passions*—these, though he tried to grasp them, were overwhelmed in the " ebullient " phrasing of Coleridge. And the meditative and retired wisdom of the pleasant senior of Pembroke, elaborated day by day with the patient travail of middle-age; his refined and fireless art; his exquisite finish, thinned out by artifice into a loss of nature; his careful effects, in which the value of each word was calculated to a grain; his eighteenth-century criticism of humanity as it was contained in his little pool of cultivated people, who were the whole world to Gray, but whom one puff of the Revolution blew into a cloudlet of spray; the soft trumpet blowing of his odes, in which long reflection is artificially wrought into an academic picture of actual human things—what comparison is there between work of that kind with this which follows, but which is built throughout on Gray?

> " Elate of heart and confident of fame,
> From vales where Avon sports the minstrel came,
>   Gay as the Poet hastes along
>   He meditates the future song,
> How Ælla battled with his country's foes:
>   And whilst Fancy in the air
>   Paints him many a vision fair,
> His eyes dance rapture, and his bosom glows."

The whole of this piece on Chatterton, written in

1790, illustrates his imitation of Gray. The recast of it, published in 1829, but done, I think, some three years later than 1790, shows him still imitating the odes of Gray. A little further on, in 1796, the *Ode to the Departing Year*, is still built on memories of Gray's manner, but the whole way of thinking is changed. Weight and reality and force, a close gaze upon the present, and a prayerful cry for the future, have replaced altogether Gray's contemplative and unimpassioned vision of the past. The old manner of Poetry is conjoined with the intensity of the new Poetry. The clothes are old, but the man in them is young. That ode holds a place exactly between the imitative and the original work of Coleridge, between the *Monody on the Death of Chatterton* and the *Ode to France*.

The "turgidity" and violence of phrase of which Coleridge was accused do not, however, appear so much in his work modelled on Gray, as in the more original poems, in the sonnets, and in such half-meta-physical and half-political poems as the *Religious Musings* and *The Destiny of Nations*. These often out-herod Herod in roaring; and I think that this is at its worst when Coleridge has some special moral or religious end in view. He had been a preacher, and in some of these early pieces there is a disagreeable note of pulpit exhortation. When a poet ex-horts, with a preacher's end in view, his imagination retires disgusted into an innermost room, and leaves the poet's work, as it left that of Coleridge, to become formless, full of effort, screaming and feeble.

Genius meets this fate when it is harnessed to any aim save an imaginative aim. It dwindles into mere talent. But the moment Coleridge, under Wordsworth's influence, began to express himself only for the pleasure he had in his emotion, or to shape the beauty he saw for the love of it alone, he ceased to be the man of talent and rose into the man of genius. I quote some lines from *Religious Musings* to illustrate into what a sad state he was betrayed—

> " From all sides rush the thirsty brood of war!—
> Austria and that foul woman of the North
> The lustful murderess of her wedded lord!
> And he, connatural Mind! whom (in their songs
> So bards of elder time had haply feigned)
> Some Fury fondled in her hate to man,
> Bidding her serpent hair in mazy surge
> Lick his young face, and at his mouth inbreathe
> Horrible sympathy! and leagued with these
> Each petty German princeling, nursed in gore!
> Soul-hardened barterers of human blood! "

As we read these terrible verses, we can scarcely believe that in a few years the same man would write the lovely simplicities of *Kubla Khan* or *The Ancient Mariner*.

However, nothing is stranger in literary history—and to say this is a truism—than the sudden leap which some of the great poets take from absurdity to power. It is only when they have proved their greatness that we know that the bellowing puffs of their youth are the unregulated outbursts of a force which is only beginning to act, and not, as in small men, the explosions of a force on the point of exhaustion. It is a young lion who is roaring in Coleridge and not a calf, but at present the sound both make is much the same. Yet, when we look back on these early poems, with the proof of the greatness of Coleridge in our hands, we find prophecies of his nobler verse in single passages, which have his special note of faery beauty, or of his imaginative quietude, or of his meditative love of nature, even of his marvellous melodies. Sometimes also, even in the midst of an explosive blast of words which in vain attempt sublimity, extraordinary lines occur; and though Imagination acts like a geyser in them, still it is Imagination. It is interesting to compare such passages in, for example, *The Destiny of Nations*, with the high and supported level of sublimity Coleridge reaches in the *Ode to France*. There is, however, beyond his growth in power, a reason in nature for the difference. In these earlier poems, such as, to instance another, *The Religious Musings*, he is speaking of abstract ideas; in the *Ode to France* of ideas embodied in actual events which rent and tore at his very life-strings. And the emotions stirred by the latter are always more powerful than those stirred by the former.

Nevertheless, Coleridge, all his life long, had the power—in a far greater degree than other poets, save perhaps Shelley—of impassionating himself about intellectual conceptions. He could have written, had not his poetic power broken down, a magnificent poem on metaphysical ideas, nor would he, like Wordsworth, have become prosaic on such subjects.

The most poetic passages in his prose-writings con-
cern such ideas—swelling, rolling, and sonorous sen-
tences, rising into an extraordinary passion of pure
thought. It is as if he beat his own mind like
a great gong into volume after volume of redundant
sound, and that the striker was his emotion and the
thunderous sound his thought. And the further
away from the material was his conception, the
more it belonged to the immeasurable, the more
impassioned he became. There is a superb instance
of this power in *Dejection*, toned down by selective
art, working unconsciously, into lovely harmonies of
rhythm and clearness of expression. In the early
poems the same kind of power is shown, but with an
unsubdued wildness in the ideas and their form.
The sound is harsh, like the gong beaten by a
Corybant. But this intellectual passion gathering
warmth around metaphysical abstractions is already
there. I quote two of these passages. Both have to
do with a favourite theory of his.

> " O! the one life within us and abroad,
>   Which meets all motion and becomes its soul.
>   A light in sound, a soundlike power in light,
>   Rhythm in all thought, and joyance everywhere—
>
> .   .   .   .   .   .
>
>   And what if all of animated nature
>   Be but organic harps diversely framed
>   That tremble into thought, as o'er them sweeps,
>   Plastic and vast, one intellectual breeze,
>   At once the Soul of each, and God of all."

The first four lines are poetry, the last five are not.

Nor are these that follow better, until they become personal. "Ebullient" is dreadful, but it well characterizes the verse.

> Contemplant Spirits, ye that hover o'er
> With untired gaze the immeasurable fount
> Ebullient with creative Deity!
> And ye, of plastic power, that interfused
> Roll through the grosser and material mass
> In organising surge! Holies of God!
>
> I haply journeying my immortal course
> Shall sometimes join your mystic choir! Till then
> I discipline my young novitiate thought
> In ministeries of heart stirring song.
> And aye on Meditation's heavenward wing
> Soaring aloft I breathe the empyreal air
> Of Love, omnific, omnipresent Love,
> Whose day-spring rises glorious in my soul
> As the great Sun, when he his influence
> Sheds on the frost-bound waters—the glad stream
> Flows to the ray and warbles as it flows."

At one point, however, in these early poems Coleridge is quite clear and simple in expression. It is when he speaks of the affections of life. Here are four lines of natural love as sweet and vivid as if Burns had written them—

> " My Sara came with gentlest look divine.
> Bright shone her eye, yet tender was its beam;
> I felt the pressure of her lip to mine!
> Whispering we went and love was all our theme.'

The lines are not unworthy of him who afterwards told in *Love* the story of romantic passion to Genevieve, but the same feeble tenderness, mixed with too pathetic a langour, which makes the questionable charm of the later poem, breathes in the rest of this early poem. There are other verses of even a greater simplicity, addressed to his domestic peace, inserted among contemplative poems like *The Æolian Harp*. But the simplicity has little intensity and no depth, and fails in natural grace. It is the want of passion in any kind of love which leaves them so uneffective; and this is a want which pervades the whole of the poetry of Coleridge. His imagination seems to leave him when his subject is the affections. He is feeble, through dreaminess, in personal love.

In fact, his Imagination was only at its height when he was away from human reality, and in the world, either of his own personality, or of the mystic realm in which *The Ancient Mariner* and *Christabel* were conceived and wrought. There are two examples among these early poems which prophesy his coming power in this sphere. One is the *Allegory of Real and Imaginary Time*. None but Coleridge could have written this; and the curious thing is, that the same note which this poem strikes in thought is heard in certain poems composed long after his singing time was past—so consistent was this subtle-woven, fine-vapoured part of his individuality, so much the child in him was father of the man.* This little poem is his metaphysic in fairy-land.

* Coleridge says that this poem, first published in 1817, was composed when he was a schoolboy, and it is included by

The other poem is *The Raven*, also first published in 1817 as a boyish poem. It is the story of the bird whose home in an old oak tree, and whose children, were destroyed by those who sacrificed the tree to build a ship. The raven lives to fly, shrieking doom and rejoicing in vengeance, over the ship as it sinks in the seas. It is the same motive, but brought out in another temper, as that of *The Ancient Mariner*—compassion and love for animals secures in the heart compassion and love for man and God. But the moral in the motive is not allowed to be dominant. The imaginative presentment of the raven is the main thing. Written when he was young, for children, he did not care, apparently, to take pains about its form, and in consequence the metrical movement is not at his highest level. The elements of any poem are so bound together that, where its conception is unfinished, the harmonies of the verse are likely to be also unequal. If we need an illustration of this we have only to think of *The Revolt of Islam*. The form of its idea is disjointed, and its melody varies as its form. And the illustration is the more effective, because Shelley, like Coleridge, was a master of poetic harmony. Nevertheless, even in its poverty, this rattling poem, *The Raven*, is an

himself among his *Juvenile Poems*. Mr Campbell, however, dates it (? 1815). I suppose he means that it was recast at that time, and this would certainly explain its elder air and its finer note. It is beautiful with the beauty of the poems of 1797.

example of that unique music of verse of which none
but Coleridge knew the spell. His metrical movement at its best is like a dance of the elemental
beings of Nature, now as of Satyrs wild round Pan;
now as of Nymphs, graceful, gay, and light as
summer leaves in the wind; now as of embodied
rivers and brooks in full and rushing joy; and now
as of Ariel and his spirits footing it featly to and fro
on the printless sands. He sang often as the winds
go, and the clouds sail, and when he sang thus, he
was at one with the life of nature, and not with the
life of man. *Kubla Khan* does not belong to human
life, and it stands alone for melody in English poetry.
Whenever Coleridge rises into this exquisite melody
in its perfection, he also rises into that subtilised
imaginative world of thought, half-supernatural,
which was special to him, and which pervades *The
Ancient Mariner* and *Christabel* and a few other
poems. The music and the sphere of the poem are
partly beyond this world of ours. Yet in part they
touch it. They belong to the nature of Titania and
Oberon, of the mysterious night, but also of the
dawn. But we, cries Oberon, are spirits of another
sort than the ghosts whom Aurora frights—

" I with the morning's love hath oft made sport,"

and sometimes the sound of them is even more un-
human, like that of the Æolian harp of which he was
so fond—

" Such a soft floating witchery of sound
    As twilight Elfins make, when they at eve

> Voyage on gentle gales from Fairy-land,
> Where melodies round honey-dropping flowers,
> Footless and wild, like birds of Paradise.
> Nor pause, nor perch, hovering on untamed wing—"

sound, wild and warbling, even disordered, yet falling into a delightsome harmony in the end,

" Till it becomes all Music murmurs of."

When the music and the imagination are perfectly married, as in *Christabel*, that music is a lovely, lonely, sweet and noticeable sound, like the singing of a bird, heard far away in the wood when all other birds are still. Or perhaps it may be better described in words from *The Ancient Mariner*, words which, in telling of the harmonies of air and earth, and then of the forest brook, image also the " sounds which delight and hurt not " in the poetry of Coleridge.

> " Sometimes a-dropping from the sky
>   I heard the skylark sing,
> Sometimes all little birds that are,
> How they seemed to fill the sea and air
>   With their sweet jargoning.
>
> And now 'twas like all instruments,
>   Now like a lonely flute;
> And now it is an angel's song
>   That makes the heavens be mute.
>
> It ceased; yet still the sails made on
>   A pleasant noise till noon,
> A noise like of a hidden brook
>   In the leafy month of June,
> That to the sleeping woods all night
>   Singeth a quiet tune."

A prophecy of this music—to try and express the beauty of which I have wearied comparison—is to be found in these early poems, in the song called *Lewti*, written in the year 1794, but inserted into the volume published in 1816. I have placed it in the following collection—though I do not care for it as a whole—because of the metrical charm and beauty of parts of it, and because these parts, even verbally, suggest not only the music but the manner of *The Ancient Mariner* when it speaks of Nature. I print here these portions of the poem—

' I saw a cloud of palest hue,
 Onward to the moon it passed;
Still brighter and more bright it grew,
With floating colours not a few,
 Till it reached the moon at last:
Then the cloud was wholly bright
With a rich and amber light!

The little cloud—it floats away,
 Away it goes; away so soon?
Alas! it has no power to stay:
Its hues are dim, its hues are grey—
 Away it passes from the moon!
How mournfully it seems to fly
 Ever fading more and more
To joyless regions of the sky—
 And now 'tis whiter than before!

I saw a vapour in the sky
 Thin and white and very high;
I ne'er beheld so thin a cloud:
 Perhaps the breezes that can fly
 Now below and now above,
Have snatched away the lawny shroud
 Of lady fair—that died for love.

> The river swans have heard my tread
> And startle from their reedy bed.
> O beauteous Birds! methinks ye measure
> Your movements to some heavenly tune!
> O beauteous Birds! 'tis such a pleasure
> To see you move beneath the moon.
> I would it were your true delight
> To sleep by day and wake all night."

Two other poems, also prophetic of a future manner, appear in the early volumes—*Lines on an Autumnal Evening*, and on *The Æolian Harp ;* and I have included the latter in these selections. The first is not good, but it is interesting. It is full of touches which belong to the poetry of the eighteenth century, and of other touches which strike chords of the New Poetry. Both poems are the first examples of the short meditative pieces in blank verse in which Nature and the human affections are gently wrought together—a special kind of poetry Coleridge may be said to have invented—and which no one has done so well.

The last thing I have to say of these early poems is that they express Coleridge's first passion for the ideas which took so intense a social and political form in the French Revolution. That great event, at its first rising, fell in disturbing and exalting power on the young poets of England. They felt France thrilling from north to south with ideas of the redemption of the human race, and they thought the ideas came from God—

> " Amid the tremor of a realm aglow,
> Amid a mighty nation jubilant,

> When from the general heart of human-kind
> Hope sprang forth like a full-born Deity!
>
> .   .   .   .   .
>
> When France in all her towns lay vibrating
> Like some becalmed bark beneath the burst
> Of Heaven's immediate thunder."

They felt this thrill in themselves. Unutterable hope and excitement set Coleridge on fire, but the fire fell as fast as it had risen. With youthful violence, with unmeasured word-painting which in a strife for sublimity becomes ridiculous, he rejoiced in the overthrow of kings, the destruction of Feudalism, the proclamation of the Rights of Man, and even, like Wordsworth, went so far as to despise and despair of England because she joined in the war against the young Republic. In what amazing English, and in what ferocious verse, he expressed this joy may be read in the one example I quote here—

> " Thus to sad sympathies I soothed my breast,
> Calm as the rainbow in the weeping West:
> When slumbering Freedom roused by high disdain
> With giant fury burst her triple chain!
> Fierce on her front the blasting Dogstar glowed,
> Her banners, like a midnight meteor, flowed;
> Amid the yelling of the storm-rent skies
> She came, and scattered battles from her eyes!
> Then exultation waked the patriot's fire
> And swept with wild hand the Tyrtean lyre;
> Red from the tyrant's wound I shook the lance
> And strode in joy the reeking plains of France."

It is to be hoped that the young lady to whom the whole of this effusion was sent, was gay enough to

smile at the image of Coleridge striding with his
bloody lance over the reeking plains. But Coleridge
had probably been reading *The Robbers* of Schiller and
sympathised with that Sturm and Drang period, when
the German poetry puts one in mind of an orchestra
made up of trombones. Coleridge soon got rid of this
gigantic manner of versing. We may well imagine
how Wordsworth laughed when he heard his friend
declaiming in this swollen fashion. Yet beneath it
there was the force of the stormy wind of genius.
Only a little temperance was necessary to make it
superb, and so it becomes in the *Ode to France*. The
loud, uplifted trumpet note of the first stanzas of
that poem, shows us what Coleridge could have done
in this Michael Angelo manner had his enthusiasms
lasted, had not his energy been so short-lived. Who
can say what the ode might not have become in his
hands!

But this is a digression. The point is that the *Ode
to France* records the passing away of the excited joy
in the French Revolution which his early poems expressed. He was always, as I said, impassioned by
ideas; but when they were stained and violated in
action, he had not the heart to cling to them. In a
mind like Coleridge's they were delicate things, and,
chilled, did not recover. It was not, however, the
conduct of the young Republic which made him sick
of humanity. It was the conduct of England. It
was not the Terror which killed his enthusiasm for
France. He had strength enough to see that after
long oppression the sun of freedom rises in crimson

clouds. But when France enslaved Switzerland, and established an Empire, he lost in this disenchantment the ideas which had enraptured him. Nor could he sever the ideas from the evil forms into which they were hurried, as a strong and steady soul would have done, as Wordsworth indeed came afterwards to do. He retreated in despair from his hopes and aims for humanity. Even humanity itself lost his interests and his thoughts. All that he had given to the outward now collected round the workings of his own soul, the metaphysical and theological problems which produce nothing but wind, and the love of quiet Nature.

The workings of his own soul supplied material for poems like the ode to *Dejection* and many others, both when he was young and in his old age. But this is not a material that endures, unless power is added to it from the emotion of the soul of the World. With it, it is true, he produced some high poetry, but lost, in losing the impassionating ideas of humanity, the capacity of continuing to produce it. The over-personal kills the power of song. I need not say that the love of metaphysical, scientific, political, and theological problems produces no poetry at all, and dries up its source. And Coleridge, knowing now what poetry was and what it was not, ceased to write verse on these problems. When then, in the absence of any large human interests, he pursued the Muse, he wrote of the world of his own soul; and when he was tired of that, of the love of quiet Nature. Before, but chiefly after, this time of disenchantment, he composed the pensive poems in blank verse, such as

Frost at Midnight, which see Nature as in a waking sleep and a sleeping dream, and over which Quiet herself folds her wing. We hear from himself that it was in this summer stillness of Nature, which answered to the warm but slumbrous love which filled him, that he now bade his heart take refuge. And there he again found Liberty.

> " And there I felt thee!—on that sea-cliff's verge,
> Where pines, scarce travelled by the breeze above
> Had made one murmur with the distant surge!
> Yes, while I stood and gazed, my temples bare,
> And shot my being through earth, sea and air,
> Possessing all things in intensest love,
> O Liberty! my spirit felt thee there."

Thus perished in a communion with the soul of Nature the wild excitement of the early poems for the ideas contained in the words Liberty, Equality, and Fraternity; and though he continued to be in his prose the warrior for spiritual freedom, he ceased to be the poet of human hopes.

The second period of Coleridge's poetic life is bound up with his meeting and friendship with Wordsworth. His influence on Wordsworth was great, and what it was is recorded in *The Prelude.* But the influence of Wordsworth on him was still greater. It was not the influence of a higher poetic imagination, for Wordsworth scarcely ever reached the imaginative beauty of which Coleridge has given us so few examples. But it was the influence of a more original, of a simpler and steadier soul on another, of one who had better principles of art rooted in him than Coleridge had

found as yet, and of one who had already re-con-
ceived and reopened the deep sources of Poetry.
Coleridge in his early poems had been like an impetuous stream forced, through artificial channels, to
move through the ordered garden of the past, rushing
and roaring against formal obstacles, angry with
its slavery, yet unable to win freedom. At last it
breaks out into the open moor. There it is itself,
and runs of its own sweet will, in simple pleasure;
natural itself, and living with Nature. It makes less
noise than before, but it enjoys its life, plays with the
flowers and stones, loves the birds and wild animals
that drink its waters, and reflects the changing sky.
This was the deliverance which came to Coleridge
from his intercourse with Wordsworth.

Wordsworth and he had then a lot divine. They
lived together in a beautiful part of Somerset, where
the soft orchard and cottage scenery ran up into the
slopes of blue hills, with meadowy hollows and
remote dells and lucent streams and wind-entangled
woods. They walked all day, chanting their runes in
gay or moralising mood, cheering each other and
cheered; their hopes, their aspirations, and their
joys the same. Their minds in difference chimed
together; each awoke the best in each; and both
were rapt by the ineffable joy of healthy youth.
Then, when the power of shaping imagination came
upon them, all the world of Nature and her beauty,
and all the world of humanity and its tenderness,
took up abode in their souls, and desired to be upon
their lips.

" That summer, under whose indulgent skies,
    Upon smooth Quantock's airy ridge we stood
    Unchecked, or loitered 'mid her sylvan combs,
    Thou in bewitching words, with happy heart,
    Didst chaunt the vision of that Ancient Man,
    The bright-eyed Mariner, and rueful woes
    Didst utter of the Lady Christabel;
    And I associate with such labour steeped
    In soft forgetfulness the livelong hours."

Out of this *The Lyrical Ballads* were born. In the
first of them, *The Ancient Mariner*, Coleridge sprang
for the first time into pure originality. We see that
Wordsworth had not only kindled, but tempered his
genius. His imitative work died, he lost his extrava-
gance, and he descended into as much reality as his
cloud-capped character would permit him to attain.
Indeed, it was impossible not to draw closer to the
simple truth of things when he lived with one who,
like Wordsworth, considered the lilies of the field as
Christ considered them, and whose joy and ardour
were like the morning. For this brief time then
Coleridge felt that rapture of life which inevitably
creates. He recovered also his youthful hopes, his
brightness of aspiration, his careless happiness, and
his belief in his genius moving the world. It is true
he fell back into depressions, but on the whole it was
May-time with him: then,

            " Life went a maying
                With Nature, hope and poesy."

" Not unhearing " did he live then

> " Of that divine and nightly-whispering voice,
> Which from my childhood to maturer years,
> Spake to me of predestinated wreaths,
> Bright with unfading colours! "

All his poems display his delight in little things—
the buoyant child,—the man who felt as a child,
playing without a care in the great hall of the
Universe.

But it did not last. He had already begun his
opium-eating, and he was too weakened by it in will
to knit himself together for the pursuit and conquest
of joy.

> " The joy within me dallied with distress.'

Soon too the power of work departed, though he
had mighty plans—"Alas! " he cries (looking back
on this period), " for the proud time when I planned,
when I had present to my mind, the materials as
well as the scheme of the hymns entitled Spirit, Sun,
Earth, Air, Water, Fire and Man, and the epic poem
on—what still appears to me the only fit subject remaining for an epic poem—Jerusalem besieged and
destroyed by Titus." Nor was his conception of
what a poet ought to be, and of a poet's work, less
exalted than his plans. He wrote to Matilda
Betham, in 1802, a poem which Mr Campbell has
rescued for us, in which the only good lines are the
following. They, in advice to this minor poetess,
describe with careful truth what makes and keeps
a poet:—

" Tho' sweet thy measures stern must be thy thoughts,
Patient thy study, watchful thy mild eye;
Poetic feelings, like the stretching boughs
Of mighty oaks, pay homage to the gales,
Toss in the strong winds, drive before the gust,
Themselves one giddy storm of fluttering leaves;
Yet, all the while, self-limited, remain
Equally near the fix'd and solid trunk
Of Truth and Nature in the howling storm,
As in the calm that stills the aspen grove.
Be bold, meek Woman! but be wisely bold!
Fly, ostrich-like, firm land beneath thy feet,
Yet hurried onward by thy wings of fancy
Swift as the whirlwind, singing in their quills.
Look round thee! look within thee! think and feel! "

The needs of poetry—great matter, lovely manner;
thought and feeling; observation of the outward,
contemplation of the inward, world; passion knit
fast to truth; peace—all are there!

Of the poems of this time *The Ancient Mariner*
and the first part of *Christabel* and *Kubla Khan* are
the most unique. *Kubla Khan* is even beyond them in
melody, but it is a fragment. They stand alone, and
all lovers of Poetry keep them in their heart. They
are as lovely as they are love-begetting, and while the
world lasts they will ravish the imagination of men.
Their music is perfect, and the spirit in them is as
akin to childhood as to age. The lover loves them
though they do not speak of love. The lover of
wisdom loves them though they do not speak of
philosophy. The lover of Nature loves them, though
they speak, only incidentally, of Nature; and all the
lovers of folklore, from those wild men who peopled
the Universe with beings who were not themselves,

to us who collect their tales that we may live in that alluring world, love them or would have loved them dearly.   *↑ opening sentence*

In *The Ancient Mariner* the events are natural, but behind them lies a supernatural world. The thoughts which Nature's powers awake in a sensitive soul are believed by Coleridge to have corresponding existences which derive their being from Nature. These bodiless beings may be felt by us as enemies or friends; and in circumstances made emotional by loneliness, they might make themselves felt as actual presences by man. But this could only be in primeval solitudes where dwell things to dream of, not to tell, or in the midst of untravelled seas, or in the deep forests of romance. In these remote mysterious seas and woods Coleridge lays the scenery of *The Ancient Mariner* and of *Christabel*. It is supernatural, but of the ancient, common, simple kind which belongs to all mankind. We feel the same thrill he desired to convey in *Christabel* if at night we are lost in a forest.

> " Like one that on a lonesome road
> Doth walk in fear and dread,
> And having once turned round, walks on,
> And turns no more his head
> Because he knows, a frightful fiend
> Doth close behind him tread."

The same expectation of the possibility of marve and horror, of mysterious sins and their forgiveness, and of the chance of meeting some forgotten spiritual life which was before man came on earth, which creeps over us as we read *The Ancient Mariner*, belongs to seamen who have been lost in unvisited spaces of ocean, vext with everlasting calm. I never met a sailor whose ship had been among the lonely places of the sea, who did not know of their hauntings, who would be surprised to see the phantom ship, who did not hear in the air that sighed in the rigging the voices of the creatures that are half of the waters and half of the air above them. With wonderful but unconscious skill Coleridge has kept this sea-poem within the limits of this subjective feeling. The supernatural in it is the translation into form of the unconscious emotions of the lonely Mariner; but all the time, in order to actualise the poem, the scenery is kept extraordinarily true to Nature. The single motive—" He prayeth well who loveth well, Both man and bird and beast,"—is so slight that it does not take the whole out of the world of dreaming phantasy, out of the mystery of the great and solitary sea; and yet, when it comes in at the end, it throws back its single impression on the whole and gives it lyric unity.

I believe this motive grew out of the poem as it went along, and that it did not form the previous basis of the poem. The only known grounds of *The Ancient Mariner* were the story of the man who in Shelvocke's Voyages shot the albatross, and a dream one of his friends told Coleridge of a ship manned by skeletons. But when the man had shot the bird of good omen, Coleridge, who hated the type of men who have no natural pity or love for the animal world, but kill from pure carelessness like a savage, imagined that the whole spiritual world of Nature would be angry with such a man because he had broken the law of love which pervaded Creation. He would then suffer many woes, but the woes would make him the apostle of pity.

So the poem is a revelation made by Coleridge of what he believed to be always the case in the spiritual world. That world is on the side of pity and love, and men who violate these are punished by hardness of heart. They cannot pray, they cannot be wise, they cannot bless the living creatures of the land and sea and sky. Nature to them is dead; and if there be powers bound up with Nature, these are their enemies till they change their hearts. And Coleridge imagined the lonesome Spirit of the South Pole who loved the Albatross, and his fellow-demons, the invisible inhabitants of the element, and the great Ocean that always looks at the moon, and the Sun and the Moon, who act with the Polar Spirit, and Death, and Life in Death,—the spiritual powers which execute the sanctions of the Law of Pity.

To support this atmosphere, in which the laws of the spiritual world take form as living beings, all the things of Nature mentioned in the poem are impersonated, have a life and will. The Storm Blast which drives the ship southward is as alive as the North Wind is in the Teuton's tale. Even the "Dark" itself comes like a giant with one stride over the sea. The water-snakes, the creatures of the calm, are full of happiness in their own beauty.

The Ocean breathes and moves and acts like one vast spirit. The Moon and the Stars have their own being, and, as if to make this plainer, Coleridge puts the thought into his prose commentary—and no lovelier little piece of imaginative prose belongs to the language—" In his loneliness and fixedness, he yearneth towards the journeying moon and the stars that still sojourn, yet still move onward; and everywhere the blue sky belongs to them, and is their appointed rest, and their native country, and their own natural homes, which they enter un-announced as lords that are certainly expected, and yet there is a silent joy at their arrival."

We are in a living world, yet as this part of the poem verges too near to the allegorical, it is so far forth removed from the mysterious in which it is con-ceived. To avoid this fault, the basis of the poem has a psychological mystery in it, such as Coleridge loved. The Ancient Mariner himself has a spiritual power which enables him to know the man to whom he must tell his tale, and who must listen to him. On this mission he wanders, with strange power of speech, from land to land. This is the actual supernatural, the spiritual Power in the poem; not allegorical, not subjective. And this it is which after all gives to the poem its deepest strangeness. All the wonders are made truly spiritual by it.

As to its poetry, it is like that of *Christabel*, not to be analysed or explained. The spirit herself of Poetry is everywhere in these two poems, felt, but never obtruding, touching spiritual life and earthly

loveliness with equal light, and so charming sens
soul with music, that what is spiritual seems sens ...,
and what is of the senses seems spiritual. And this
inability to define the poetic beauty of these poems
is more felt when we read *Christabel* than when we
read *The Ancient Mariner*. It is in a critic's power
to analyse the unearthly music of *Kubla Khan*, but
I defy the whole body of critics to analyse the music
of the first part of *Christabel*. It belongs to the
imagination as much as the vision of the poem itself.
It is almost a pity—save for a few passages—that
the second part was ever written afterwards. The
ineffable element has fled from it. The subject
presented itself, when first conceived, to Coleridge
as a whole. He saw it from beginning to end. It
was then he should have written it all, while he still
lived in the dim country of the creatures who are
neither of earth nor of heaven, while he still possessed
the faery music. Short was that time; and so fine
and rare were the sound and the thought of the
examples we have of its arch-faery poetry, that he
never seems to have been able to finish them. He,
with his ear, and with his imagination, (which
lasted in feeling, but had lost its shaping power),
knew better than any one that he could not recover
the immeasurable hour when he wrote these things,
or when they wrote themselves, when

> " he on honey-dew had fed,
> And drank the milk of Paradise."

The projected poem on *The Wanderings of Cain*

is also a fragment, and, if we may trust the lovely
prose of its projection, would have been a master-
piece. Scarcely a dozen lines, which have some of
the quality and melody of *Christabel*, represent it.

> " Encinctured with a twine of leaves,
> That leafy twine his only dress,
> A lovely boy was plucking fruits
> By moonlight in a wilderness.—
> The moon was bright, the air was free,
> And fruits and flowers together grew
> On many a shrub and many a tree:
> And all put on a gentle hue,
> Hanging in the shadowy air
> Like a picture rich and rare.
> It was a climate where they say
> The night is more belov'd than day.
> But who that beauteous boy beguil'd
> That beauteous boy to linger here?
> Alone by night, a little child,
> In place so silent and so wild—
> Has he no friend, no loving mother near? " *

* The prose of what he was to do in poetry I have put into
a note on the poem at the end of this book. It is a curious
piece, and it would have been of his most special imaginative
quality had he put it into verse. It also hovers in the world
between the human and dæmonic, in the sense in which
Goethe used that word. Whether Abel is, in Coleridge's
mind, really Abel, or a false image of him which is to lead
Cain into deeper sorrow, I cannot tell; but the motive towards the end of the fragment, in which Abel in misery pro-
claims a God of the dead different from the God of the living,
and sets Cain into wonder and question, is full mysticism.
The fragment is like a piece out of Blake, and might have
been written by him. It adds another story to the story
in the Bible, and adds it in contradiction of the New
Testament conception of Abel.

Another curious thing is that here, and in another place—

Quite different from these mystic poems are certain quiet, simple, meditative poems of which, as I said, *The Æolian Harp* in the early poetry is the ante-type. He calls one of them—*The Nightingale* —a " Conversation-poem," and they are conversations with himself about Nature and humanity. They are written in a feeble, wandering blank-verse, a metre which Coleridge never mastered; but the verse seems to suit their dreamy sauntering. They are all born and nursed in solitude; when he is left alone in the *Lime-tree Bower*, or in a green and silent spot among the hills, or by his fireside on a frosty night, or in a walk from vale to vale, or under the stars in a quiet hour when he recalls how Wordsworth, he, and Dorothy listened to the nightingale. They are full of contemplative painting of Nature in her pensive moods, full of the " harvest of a quiet eye," which sees the smallest thing that has charm, and loves it, but sees all under a low, soft, moonlit light, in a veiled music. Nature does not occupy them altogether. Memory floats into the poem, and Coleridge thinks of his own past, and then from him-

The Blossoming of the Solitary Date Tree—Coleridge writes a prose analysis of the poem he is about to make, a process so unlike a poet's way that it confounds us with its strangeness. A poet thinks his poem in metre, or rather in poetry. To translate it from prose into poetry, to conceive a subject in prose and then to reconceive it in poetry, and to do this deliberately, prophesies that Coleridge would soon cease to write poetry, so radically apart, both in origin and method, are Prose and Poetry. All marriage between them is completely detestable.

self glides to his friends, to his child, and to the Master of the soul. The prevalent note of quiet is never violated; the temperature of feeling is always the same. It is curious to contrast them with the fire and the loud sea-noise of poems like the *Ode to France*, and their slow, humming blank-verse with the wildering dulcimers of *Christabel*.

One thing is especially remarkable in these meditative poems. It is their frequent use of phrases and thoughts which we might say belong to Wordsworth. I quote a few of these.

> " Henceforth I shall know
> That Nature ne'er deserts the wise and pure;
> No plot so narrow, be but Nature there,
> No waste so vacant, but may well employ
> Each faculty of sense, and keep the heart
> Awake to Love and Beauty!

>   Sea and hill and wood
> With all the numberless goings on of life
> Inaudible as dreams.

> And grateful that by Nature's quietness,
> And solitary musings, all my heart
> Is softened, and made worthy to indulge
> Love, and the thoughts that yearn for human kind.

> The sunny showers, the dappled sky,
> The little birds that warble high,
>   Their vernal loves commencing,
> Will better welcome you than I,
>   With their sweet influencing.

> Poet, who hath been building up the rhyme
> When he had better far have stretched his limbs

> Beside a brook in mossy forest dell,
> By sun or moonlight, to the influxes
> Of shapes and sounds and shifting elements
> Surrendering his whole spirit, of his song
> And of his fame forgetful! So his fame
> Should share in Nature's immortality
> A venerable thing! and so his song
> Should make all Nature lovelier, and itself
> Be loved like Nature.

> *   *   *   *   *   *

> If so he might not wholly cease to be,
> He would far rather not be that he is;
> But would be some thing that he knows not of,
> In winds or waters or among the rocks! "

These are thoughts phrased by the communion those two wondrous creatures had when they walked together

> " On seaward Quantock's heathy hills,"

and Dorothy encompassed them with her love and ardour,—" three people with one soul."

The last of these poems in date—*The Nightingale* with the poem of *Love*—both of them in 1798-99—mark the close of the vivid and productive time of Coleridge as a poet. His southern association with the Wordsworths was broken up. He separated from them in Germany, and when he rejoined them, in that continuous intercourse of which Dorothy Wordsworth tells so much in her diary kept at Dove Cottage, he had lost his poetic energy, had, indeed, in 1800 " abandoned poetry," he says, " being convinced that I never had the essentials of a poet's genius." But this conviction arose out of the con-

fusion and disgust of life caused by opium, of which
drug he now began to make a continuous use. That
his poetical power was only in abeyance, and could
be summoned when he wished, is proved by *Dejection—an Ode*, written in 1802, a storehouse of
splendid poetry, set to wild and changeful music. It
is at once the proof that he could write poems as
well as ever, and the image of a soul which had lost
the power to write it continuously. There is no need
to speak of it; it is in itself the closest self-revelation
almost ever written. Only one other poem of his is
more sorrowful, more like despair, more self-reveal-
ing—the poem addressed in 1807 to Wordsworth
after reading *The Prelude*. Nevertheless, during this
time, and especially when he was with the Wordsworths, he was not all dejection. There were times
when he felt enough to command the whole of
poetry. In 1803 he writes—" I never find myself
alone within the embracement of rocks and hills, . . .
but my spirit careers, drives, and eddies, like a leaf
in autumn, a wild activity of thoughts, imaginations, feelings, and impulses of motion rises up
within me. . . . The further I ascend from animated
nature . . . the greater in me becomes the intensity
of the feeling of life. Life seems to me then a
universal spirit, that neither has nor can have an
opposite ! God is everywhere, and where is there
room for death ? "

This is the picture of a poet, but his emotion was
rarely strong enough to stir his imagination into

shaping with joy and power what he felt. *The Hymn before Sunrise in the Valley of Chamouni* belongs to this time, but, fine as it is, it is over-wrought and over-worded. That it was an enlargement of German stanzas by Frederike Brun, shows how little now he cared to find subjects out of his own soul. Indeed, he was never at Chamouni in his life, and the poem is really lifeless. The *Inscription for a Fountain on a Heath* is lovely, but the other fine things of this time are almost all records of distress and hopelessness and bitter misery. No one has written better, as *The Pains of Sleep* will prove, of personal and tortured wretchedness. In the midst of this it is wonderful to come, in 1815, upon the two songs in *Zapolya*, so beautiful that I think they must belong to the earlier time, and been introduced into this Drama. In 1816-17, a wish to write poetry again seems to have glided into his will, but it died away, and after that only a few things (among which is that perfect flower of poetry, *Youth and Age*), mark at long intervals that he was once a poet, and might have endured a poet. What he had been, seemed to float sometimes before his eyes. He once saw in vision the spiritual being of his youth, long since gone away to heaven, come down to visit him in 1830. But when it had wooed its way into his soul, it did not recognise its surroundings, and " shrank back, like one that had mistook," and in its eyes

" That weary, wandering, disavowing look."

And he himself, though he knew it was his own spirit, saw that it was also " All another " than himself, " feature, look, and frame." " O to what," cries his friend to whom he told the vision, " does this riddling tale belong? "

> " Is't history? vision? or an idle song?
>   Or rather say at once, within what space
>   Of time this wild disastrous change took place? "

And Coleridge answers—

> " Call it a *moment's* work (and such it seems)—
>   This tale's a fragment from the life of dreams;
>   But say, that years matured the silent strife,
>   And 'tis a record from the dream of life! "

This is the little poem *Phantom and Fact*, written three years before his death; and it is the piteous quintessence of years of brooding regret.

The poem that follows, *Love's Apparition and Banishment*, is equally sorrowful, and its first two lines paint Coleridge in these hours of retrospection and old age under a comparison he has used before.

> " Like a lone Arab, old and blind,
>   Some caravan had left behind—"

But it would be to picture him untruly to say that these hours or their temper were continuous. He was not without pleasure, manliness, faith or hope, and love was always his. 'Twas a mixed close. Though earth, sea and sky should make war against him, and try to end his life, the breath of the true life he still drew, he vows, in Christ. Death dies, he says, at the death-bed. Nor is it without a memory, sad but not now despairing, of the short and sunny time when he was a great singer that he speaks his last verses in his epitaph—

> " Beneath this sod
> A poet lies, or that which once seemed he.—"

When the close of life drew near, he thus forgot his prose, and remembered his poetry; and in the years to come, when all the controversies on which he wrote have lost their worth and interest in a greater and simpler light, it will be thus with the world of men. They will forget his prose; they never will forget him as a poet.

The position of Coleridge with regard to the two great subjects which awaken the imagination of poets—human nature and outward nature—was a curious position. He does not seem to have felt the affairs of either one or the other with the intensity of the other poets of this century. Indeed, as long as he worked on the actual, he had no passion in his work. *His* imagination was only wrought into high activities in that world where Man and Nature are of the stuff which dreams are made of.

As to human affairs, it may be said that his enthusiasm for the Revolution shared in passion. But it had not the enduringness of true emotion. It was easily chilled, and its voice came in gusty and violent squalls that carried with them the doom of their own transiency. No one was ever more like Hamlet than Coleridge in his mingling of philosophy with poetry, in his sudden outbreaks of energy, and in their conclusion of words, only words; and like Hamlet he knew well that these transient energies were not the children of steady passion. No one might have repeated with more fitness, with regard to his excitement for humanity, the speech of Hamlet's beginning—

" Why, what a rogue and peasant slave am I! "

And no one has recorded this more clearly. Like Hamlet then, he lost his imaginary passion for men, first in violent words, and then in meandering thought on side issues, until many idle, flitting phantasies had like clouds veiled and then obscured the original thought and its original emotion.

The same want of all that we call passion affects his treatment of the ordinary affections of humanity. He is tender in them, quiet, pensive, gentle, but never intense. The poem entitled *Love*, in which he sings the wooing of a maid by a man, illustrates what I say. It is soft, pathetic, even warm, but it has no fire; and this is the reason why among his finer poems it takes only a second place. The few poems addressed to Mary Evans, the subject of his only romantic love, try to express a great deal, but do not succeed. He drifts away from love into phantasies of thought, as Hamlet from Ophelia. The poems to Sara, his wife, are commonplace; but then he had not much care for her. Indeed,

I do not think he ever truly loved a woman. paternal love seems to reach a greater fulness of feeling in the meditative poems, but it was not deep or strong. It also floats away into a musing contemplation. Friendship, that quiet, still-voiced thing, did most with him, and was most felt, but even it was subject to vicissitude. Even the friendship which breathes so deeply through his poems to Wordsworth, even the egotistic sentiment he felt for Dorothy, rose and fell in jets, and once at least disappeared. But while he had no intensity in any of these affections, the pensive, gentle lovingness of his nature was always steady, always full, always grateful for love. He did not then love passionately, but he loved far and wide, and tenderly.

Something of the same wants and the same softness prevails in his love of Nature, as shown in his poetry. In his philosophy of Nature, at the time in his life when Philosophy bore no other name but Poesy, he felt a living spirit in Nature, but it was the human soul of the watcher of Nature which filled the world with life.

> " O lady, we receive but what we give,
> And in our life alone doth Nature live."

Even the influence of Nature on us drew its main power over us from the spirit that contemplated it. He thought

> " That outward forms, the loftiest still receive
> Their finer influences from the life within."

But this half-philosophy, which is fully expanded in the *Ode to Dejection*, did not always master his perception of Nature. He was often sufficiently influenced by Wordsworth to adopt, or to seem to adopt, his view of Nature as something separate from us whose soul might be thought to communicate with ours. To him then, as to Wordsworth, Nature brought healing and sweet changes—

> " With other ministrations thou, O Nature!
> Healest thy wandering and distempered child:
> Thou pourest on him thy soft influences,
> Thy sunny hues, fair forms, and breathings sweet,
> Thy melodies of woods, and winds and waters,
> Till he relent, and can no more endure
> To be a jarring and a dissonant thing
> Amid this general dance and minstrelsy;
> But, bursting into tears, wins back his way,
> His angry spirit healed and harmonized
> By the benignant touch of love and beauty."

This is pure Wordsworth, and many other verses tell the same story. Nature " awakes the sense to love and beauty." She " softens the heart till it is worthy to love man." She " never deserts the wise and pure." She " converses with the mind and gives it

> ' A livelier impulse and a dance of thought.' "

She charms men into union with herself, till those who love her share in her immortality and their work becomes a part of Nature, and is loved like Nature.

Man and Nature pass into one another in cea[ ]
interchange. Nature educates the child; the bo[ ]
her playmate, and all her education is God's eternal
language—

> " But thou, my babe, shalt wander like a breeze
> By lake and sandy shore, beneath the crags
> Of ancient mountains, and beneath the clouds,
> Which image in their bulk both lakes and shores,
> And mountain crags: so shalt thou see and hear
> The lovely shapes and things intelligible
> Of that eternal language which thy God
> Utters, who from eternity doth teach
> Himself in all, and all things in himself."

These views of Nature, as I have said in another
connection, are Wordsworth in Coleridge; but for
the most part Nature in the poetry of Coleridge is
mingled with his moods, takes the note of his transient feeling; or, to put it otherwise, he chooses such
things in Nature as are in tune with his soul, and then
fuses himself and Nature both together into one imagination. Some of the best lyrics in the world, and
notably Shelley's *Ode to the West Wind*, are done in
this fashion.

Except for a short period, these moods in which
Coleridge saw Nature were those of saddened
thought, the thought of failure, and of knowledge
that he was too languid to overcome failure—a
" wan and heartless mood." Sometimes the mood
was more dreamy than sad, with drifting thought
into which " the one life within us and abroad "
flowed and flowed out again, creating joy as it passed,

and melancholy as it passed away, but not creating thought, only an idle tangle of phantasy. He loved to lie, high on the hills, surrendering his spirit to the shifting elements of Nature's movement, of song and fame forgetful, his eyes half-closed with pleasure, floating in a dream which was half of opium and half of the delight which comes of hushing the will to sleep.

But always there was, even in the profoundest dejection, a subtle though slumbrous sense and love of the beauty of the world, a capacity for enjoying it in little things as well as great, and an equal capacity for selecting remote and fine specialities of beauty, such as pleased his soul in super-subtle hours. This deep love of the beauty of the universe never failed him, nor his sense of joy in it. The little poem *To Nature*, speaks of the deep and inward joy in created things which closely clings to his heart. The immortal spirit of Love in nature dwelt in him, and touches, to the end, his Nature-poetry. Nor did there ever fail in him that feeling of Beauty which is the source of love, nor the divine results which flow into the soul from both. What his Ancient Mariner felt, he felt all his life long for Man and beast, for all the Universe—

> O happy living things! no tongue
> Their beauty might declare:
> A spring of love gushed from my heart,
> And I blessed them unaware:
> Sure my kind saint took pity on me
> And I blessed them unaware.

Even in old age beauty awoke his ardour, and there is no more delightful proof of this than his poem written in 1828, *The Garden of Boccaccio*, where the love, the joyaunce and the gallantry of the *Decameron*, brings back to him all spirits of power that most had stirred his thought in boyhood, and charmed his youth; and where the verse flows light and gay and rejoicing from the momentary hour, in which, age forgotten, loveliness has made the philosopher again the poet.

The Natural Description which partly grew out of this poetic philosophy of Nature, and partly out of this dreamy perception of beauty, passed, I may say, through three phases; only the last of which was characterized by intensity of imagination. In the first of these phases, which belongs chiefly to his earlier poetry, his natural description is quite uncomposed. It resembles a catalogue of the different things he sees as he takes his walk. The lines composed while climbing *Brockley Coomb*, and those addressed to Charles Lloyd, are of this kind; describing step by step what strikes the eye as he climbs the steep moors—isolated images touched with fancy, but bound together by no imagination into a whole, and uninfluenced by any creative passion—until he reaches the top of the hill, when the vision of the great landscape below opens his heart to strong emotion and opens his verse:

" Dim coasts, and cloud-like hills, and shoreless ocean—
    It seemed like omnipresence!   God, methought,

Had built him there a temple: the whole world
Seemed imaged in its vast circumference:
No *wish* profaned my overwhelmed heart.'

But for the most part all the verses of this earlier
time which describe Nature, are devoid of any strong
emotion.   Stranger still, they want any of those sur-
prising or intimate touches of Nature, those happy
words, even that melody which is like the melody
of Nature itself, in which he afterwards excelled.   A
few phrases like the music of—

"By lonely Otter's sleep-persuading stream,"

or "the night was fanged with frost," awake our
pleasure, but they are astonishingly few.   The one
exception are the lovely lines I have already quoted
from the *Circassian Love-Chant*, about the clouds
and the moon and the swans on the river.

The second phase appears in those poems which
contemplate and describe Nature in a resting and
meditative temper.   There is no passionate feeling in
their delight.   The joy he has in the beauty of the
world is the joy of dreaming, often only a recollected
joy in what he has seen.   He found in poems of this
class one of the natural paths of his imagination,
and in the earliest of them he for the first time
becomes an artist.   Their pensiveness, their dying
fall, their self-loving melancholy are harmonized by
him with Nature.   He chiefly chooses for their
scenery some delightful evening, pale and calm, or

the swimming vision of the earth in moonlight.
The moon indeed belongs to Coleridge's soul. No
one has ever described moonshine so well. Their
quietude is increased by most of them being written,
not direct from Nature, but from pictures made
when he sits alone at home—" My eyes," he says,
" make pictures when they're shut." In *Frost at
Midnight* he watches while he sits by the fire all the
secret ministry of Frost weaving its web outside,
while he weaves his own web of memory within.
In *The Lime-tree Bower my Prison*, he follows the
landscape in which his friends are walking, and
describes it from memory while he lies quiet, and
then with an unusual turn records with delightful
minuteness exactly what he sees as he looks up
through the sun-besprinkled leaves—

> " and I watched
> Some broad and sunny leaf, and loved to see
> The shadow of the leaf and stem above,
> Dappling its sunshine ! "—

a piece of delicate description as fine as Wordsworth's " The daisy's shadow on the naked stone."
And it would be hard to match in this kind of poetry,
where contemplation watches the world through
Slumber's half-closed eyes, the beginning of *Fears
in Solitude* ; or the lyric image of the same moorland,
seen as he lay on the couch of dreamy memory, and
yet alive to the travelling of the most delicate sounds
in Nature—

" Eight springs have flown, since last I lay
   On seaward Quantock's heathy hills,
   Where quiet sounds from hidden rills
   Float here and there, like things astray,
   And high o'erhead the sky-lark shrills."

These minute and delicate sights and sounds are
common in Coleridge. The scent of the bean field:
the peculiar tint of yellow green which rarely occurs
at sunset, the solitary red leaf dancing in the wind on
the top of the oak, the slip of smooth clear blue
betwixt two isles of purple shadow, the constelled
stars of the foam darting off into the darkness, the
tiny cone of sand which soundless dances at the
bottom of the spring, the twofold sound of the rain,
the sunny islands on the dark mountain side, the
imagined star within the nether tip of the moon, and
many other fine-seen things, were impulses that like
wafts of wind made the whole surface of his sense
of beauty ripple with pleasant and tiny waves. In
truth, contemplative hours, in which imagination
only simmers, lend themselves to these minute
observances of Nature. But they cannot produce
those higher generalizations of the beauty of earth or
sky or sea in which the soul plays so great a part,
which flash forth a whole scene or a whole element
in a few lines, and in which the imagination works
like a swift-dealing smith on white-hot material—
generalizations such as Coleridge makes in another
class of poems. Here is one of them, of the coming
of a phantom hurricane, every line true to Nature.
yet greater than Nature herself—

The upper air burst into life!
   And a hundred fire-flags sheen,
To and fro they were hurried about!
And to and fro, and in and out,
   The wan stars danced between.

And the coming wind did roar more loud
   And the sails did sigh like sedge;
And the rain poured down from one black cloud:
   The moon was at its edge.

The thick black cloud was cleft, and still
   The moon was at its side;
Like waters shot from some high crag,
The lightning fell with never a jag,
   A river steep and wide.

This is the third phase of his natural description, and he works there in his world of dreams, among

" The Power, the Beauty, and the Majesty
   That had their haunts in dale or piny mountain,
Or forest by slow stream, or pebbly spring,
Or chasms or watery depths."

In this world he *does* reach passionate description of Nature, but in it the natural scenery is never alone. It is thrilled through and through with that subtle wanderer, Coleridge. In it his imagination rises to its highest peak, and commands humanity and Nature, and the most delicate music of both. This is the world in which arises Alph the sacred river, and the gardens and forests of Kubla Khan, and the deep romantic chasm, holy and enchanted, and the dome of pleasure, and the Abyssinian maid, singing of Mount Abora. This is the world in which the upper air bursts into life, in which the sky is full of the sweet jargoning of birds, in which the hidden brook sings its quiet tune all night to the woods. This is the world of *The Ancient Mariner*, and of those descriptions of sky and sea in storm and calm and mist, of the rising moon and setting sun, of moonlight on the charmed sea, of moonlight in the harbour of home, which are each complete wholes, true to Nature, yet alive with being above Nature, and which Imagination herself can never forget. They are chosen for their strangeness; and a certain spiritual mystery, as if they were commanded from another world for a purpose, is just touched into them. Above all, they are felt with a passion extraordinary in Coleridge, and which, in the desire of passion to get to the simplest expression of the essential fact, has rejected all that is superfluous.

Nor in this class of poem is human feeling less strongly felt. The extremity of fear was never better pictured than in these lines—

> " We listened and looked sideways up;
> Fear at my heart, as at a cup
> My life-blood seemed to sip! "

The joy of sleep cannot be more simply, yet intensely given than in these lovely lines—

> " O Sleep! it is a gentle thing
> Beloved from pole to pole!
> To Mary Queen the praise be given!
> She sent the gentle sleep from heaven,
> That slid into my soul."

And loneliness, the solitude of the soul of ma̅ ̅ ̅ ̅
sorrow, has chosen as its best expression the cry of
this restless Mariner—

> " O Wedding Guest! this soul hath been
> Alone on a wide wide sea.
> So lonely 'twas that God himself
> Scarce seemed there to be."

Nor is the exquisite joy of his return to home less
close to the heart of man. But, as usual when Coleridge is writing at this high level, we are content
with the pleasure of it. The natural scenery in
Christabel, the oaks, the red leaves, the moonlight,
the forest, are only indicated, but they fill the
imagination. Of the same class, but at a lower level,
is the little bit of sun and shade in *The Three Graves*.
The suppressed supernaturalism, the outside-the-
world psychology of Coleridge has entered into
Nature, and the scene is thrilled with imaginative
elements. The extreme simplicity of the description,
as of those descriptions in *The Ancient Mariner*,
heighten this effect of mystery, nor can anyone
mistake its intensity.

> " No path leads thither, 'tis not nigh
>   To any pasture plot;
> But clustered near the chattering brook
>   Some hollies marked the spot.
> Those hollies of themselves a shape
>   As of an arbour took,
> A close, round arbour; and it stands
>   Not three strides from a brook.
> Within this arbour, which was still
>   With scarlet berries hung,

Where these three friends, one Sunday morn
    Just as the first bell rung.
'Tis sweet to hear a brook, 'tis sweet
    To hear the Sabbath bell,
'Tis sweet to hear them both at once
    Deep in a woody dell.

.   .   .   .   .

The sun peeps through the close thick leaves,
    See, dearest Ellen, see!
'Tis in the leaves, a little sun,
    No bigger than your ee;
A tiny sun, and it has got
    A perfect glory too:
Ten thousand threads and hairs of light
Make up a glory gay and bright
    Round that small orb, so blue."

But it was not only in this mystic outer world that
he reached passion and his highest level of imaginative power. There was another world more mystic
still, the dim, supernatural world of his own soul. In
this world, *The Ode to Dejection, The Pains of Sleep,
Youth and Age,* and other poems were written. Every
description of Nature in the Ode to Dejection is
penetrated with the mystic temper of his inner life,
and the natural things he speaks of have become part
of the landscape of his heart. The crescent moon
with the old moon in her arms, the sunset bars, the
clouds that give away their motion to the stars, the
rising gale, the outburst of the storm raving over
crags and pines and gardens, are all in his own
thought-entangled heart, and derive their passionate
expression from the restless world within him. He
is the mad Lutanist whose name he gives to the

wind, as Shelley himself changes into the west wind at the end of that poem.

To what powers of natural description of the more real world, unaffected by psychology, he might also have won his way, I cannot tell; but the extraordinary excellence of the drawing of Nature in these Other-world poems predicts what he could have done, had he cared to bestow travail upon his art. And there are a few verses, not contemplative and not mixed up with human or faery mystery, which describe Nature directly and with loss of self in her. The poem adapted from the German, and which he calls *Catullian Hendecasyllables*, is one of the most brilliant descriptions in the language. The *Inscription for a Fountain on a Heath* is done with crystal clearness of sight and words, and touches the edge of Fairyland. The little translation from Stolberg, *On a Cataract*, has lines in it, not in the German, which are so like Shelley's work on pure Nature that we say—if Coleridge could have let himself loose, he might have anticipated Shelley whose music he even excelled.

> " There's a cloud at the portal, a spray-woven veil
>   At the shrine of his ceaseless renewing;
> It embosoms the roses of dawn,
> It entangles the shafts of the noon,
> And into the bed of its stillness
> The moonshine sinks down as in slumber,
> That the son of the rock, that the nursling of Heaven
> May be born in a holy twilight! "

These several poems are outside of the phases of

which I have spoken, and each of them stands alone, is of a separate kind in poetry.

What a regret it is that he was so wrangled by the fate which made him bewildered in life that he could not pursue these separate kinds of poetry, and instead of one example of each bestow upon us fifty! He tried others also, and succeeded when he tried. The political denunciation of Pitt is fiercer and more vigorous than anything of Byron's. The translation of *Wallenstein* stands alone among translations. Such an adaptation of a heavy German poem as *The Hymn in the Valley of Chamouni* only makes us regret that he wasted on adaptations, better however than any-one else could have done, powers which might have been employed in original work. But it suited his laziness to have a subject given to him rather than to create a subject. His epigrams are good, but they cannot compare with Landor's; and lastly, it is curious that the delicate and pensive poet of the contemplative poems, the poet of *Christabel* and *The Ancient Mariner*, of imagination all compact, should be able to write with so much force verses of rough, slashing, and even coarse humour—such verses as the sonnet on the *House that Jack built*, and the *Two round spaces on the Tombstone*. In many forms of poetry he could work better than others—in none did he grant to us more than three or four ex-amples. But let us say grace for those we have received, enjoy them, love them, and honour the Poet.

Lastly, when we wish to see Coleridge kindly—
and the sight of kindness is the truest—there is no
judgement on him better than that made by the
friend who knew him in his brilliant youth, and in
his broken years; who spent day after day with him
on the hills of Somerset: who walked and sat with
him for hours at Dove Cottage; who wandered with
him in the trying companionship of summer tours;
who, though there was once a disagreement, cherished with him an unbroken friendship till death
parted them from one another; and who, in lines
which touch the notes of his ancient power,
records in 1835 how undiminished by age and
weakness was the impression of Coleridge on
Wordsworth—

> Nor has the rolling year twice measured,
> From sign to sign, its steadfast course,
> When every mortal power of Coleridge
> Was frozen at its marvellous source;
>
> The rapt one with the godlike forehead,
> The Heaven-eyed creature sleeps in earth:

Many books, letters, and diaries speak of this long
admiration and love between these two, and Coleridge expresses it fully in his poem made after reading *The Prelude*. As to Wordsworth's love of his
friend, it is more beautifully disclosed in the *Stanzas*
written in his copy of the *Castle of Indolence* than in
any book, letter, or journal. It was delighted

and delightful happiness with one another.* " He,"
that is Coleridge—

> He would entice that other Man to hear
> His music, and to view his imagery;
> And, sooth, these two were to each other dear:
> No livelier love in such a place could be:
> There did they dwell †—from earthly labour free,
> As happy spirits as were ever seen;
> If but a bird, to keep them company,
> Or butterfly sate down, they were, I ween,
> As pleased as if the same had been a Maiden Queen.

In the same poem, written in 1802, Wordsworth
describes the figure and ways of Coleridge—

> With him there often walked in friendly guise,
> Or lay upon the moss by brook or tree,
> A noticeable Man with large grey eyes,
> And a pale face that seemed undoubtedly
> As if a blooming face it ought to be;

---

* When Wordsworth writes about his wanderings before
he met Coleridge, he loves him so much that he places him
among them—

> O Friend! we had not seen thee at that time,
> And yet a power is on me, and a strong
> Confusion, and I seem to plant thee there.
> Far art thou wandered now in search of health
> And milder breezes—melancholy lot!
> But thou art with us, with us in the past,
> The present, with us in the days to come,
> There is no grief, no sorrow, no despair,
> No languor, no dejection, no dismay,
> No absence scarcely can there be, for those
> Who love as we do.

† In Dove Cottage, Grasmere.

Heavy his low-hung lip did oft appear,
Deprest by weight of musing Phantasy;
Profound his forehead was, yet not severe;
Yet some did think that he had little business here.

Sweet heaven forefend! his was a lawful right;
Noisy he was, and gamesome as a boy:
His limbs would toss about him with delight
Like branches when strong winds the trees annoy.
Nor lacked his calmer hours device or toy
To banish listlessness and irksome care;
He would have taught you how you might employ
Yourself; and many did to him repair,—
And certes not in vain, he had inventions rare.

Expedients, too, of simplest sort he tried:
Long blades of grass, plucked round him as he lay
Made, to his ear attentively applied,
A pipe in which the wind would deftly play;
Glasses he had, that little things display,
The beetle panoplied in gems and gold,
A mailed angel on a battle-day;
The mysteries that cups of flowers enfold,
And all the gorgeous sights that fairies do behold.

This is a very different image of Coleridge from that described by Carlyle. That indeed was drawn of him in his old age when Philosophy had made him older than he ought to have been, and by the hand of cynicism. Wordsworth's is the image of his youth when Poetry had made him as young as he is in Heaven; and it was drawn by the hand of love. We will keep the one and ignore the other, or if we wish to contrast the age of Coleridge with his youth, we will do it as he has done it himself in his poem of

Youth and Age. There we shall feel the poet still, and there remember

> The wizard song, the Charmer and his charms.

With this deep-set joy of heart, and gaiety of body, Wordsworth harmonizes, in *The Prelude*, the still rapture of Coleridge in beauty seen, and then imagined from the seen into its unseen ideal, and his lovingness of nature, gentler than that of all other men. This lovingness made his sympathy unfailing, his judgements never harsh. " O capacious soul," cries Wordsworth—

> Placed on this earth to love and understand,
> And from thy presence shed the light of love!

It was this rejoicing love of all things, in which Wordsworth also shared, this tender gentleness of which Wordsworth had but little, rather than Coleridge's intellect, which made him the special power he was in the history of Thought, which made Wordsworth class him with himself, with all poets who loved much, as a Prophet of Nature, that is, of the Nature of Man and of the Universe.—" What we have loved," he says—

> Others will love and we will teach them how,
> Instruct them how the mind of man becomes
> A thousand times more beautiful than the earth
> On which he dwells—

Nor does Wordsworth speak less strongly of the intellectual power of his friend. It was Coleridge, he

said, who brought the thoughts and things of the
self-haunting spirit of his youth into rational pro-
portions, and the mysteries of life and death, time
and eternity into close connection with humanity;
balancing the supersensuous imaginations, which
belong to them, by pathetic truth, by trust in hope-
ful reason, and by reverence for duty. It is a work
which Coleridge, more by the spirit of his nature
than by his reasonings, has done for many others.
No praise seems too great for Wordsworth to use of
Coleridge's intellectual power when he knew him in
those early days.

> I have thought
> Of thee, thy learning, gorgeous eloquence,
> And all the strength and plumage of thy youth;
> Thy subtle speculations, toils abstruse
> Among the schoolmen, and Platonic forms
> Of wild ideal pageantry, shaped out
> From things well-matched or ill, and words for things;
> The self-created sustenance of a mind
> Debarred from Nature's living images,
> Compelled to be a life unto herself,
> And unrelentingly possessed by thirst
> Of greatness, love, and beauty.

With these came " rigorous study," till he could say
that Coleridge had " trod a march of glory." But
science and intellectual power were not, Wordsworth thought, all in all to Coleridge. They were but
handmaids in his mind to that higher power by
which we are finally made free to love that spiritual
Love which acts through imagination.

Which, in truth
Is but another name for absolute power
And clearest insight, amplitude of mind,
And Reason in her most exalted mood.

Hence, though Coleridge loved to analyse, his friend
declared he was no slave to analysis, "that secondary
power by which we multiply distinctions" and deem
that they are truths, and not things which we our-
selves have made, in and for the transitory.

This was Wordsworth's view of the intellectual
power of his friend; and how, combined with essential
love, it emerged in the poetry of Coleridge, is best
described in the magnificent lines in *The Prelude*
where Wordsworth speaks of the great Nature which
exists in the works of " mighty poets "—

Visionary power
Attends the motives of the viewless winds,
Embodied in the mystery of words:
There darkness makes abode, and all the host
Of shadowy things work endless changes,—there
As in a mansion like their proper home,
Even forms and substances are circumfused
By that transparent veil with light divine,
And, through the turnings intricate of verse,
Present themselves as objects recognized,
In flashes, and with glory not their own.

I.

MEDITATIVE POEMS

THE EOLIAN HARP.

COMPOSED AT CLEVEDON, SOMERSETSHIRE.

pensive Sara! thy soft cheek reclined
as on mine arm, most soothing sweet it is
sit beside our cot, our cot o'ergrown
h white-flowered Jasmin, and the broad-leaved
  Myrtle,
et emblems they of Innocence and Love!),
d watch the clouds, that late were rich with light,
w saddening round, and mark the star of eve
enely brilliant (such should wisdom be)
ne opposite! How exquisite the scents
tched from yon bean-field! and the world so hushed!
e stilly murmur of the distant sea
ls us of silence.

         And that simplest lute,
ced length-ways in the clasping casement, hark!
w by the desultory breeze caressed,
e some coy maid half yielding to her lover,
pours such sweet upbraiding, as must needs
mpt to repeat the wrong! And now, its strings
dlier swept, the long sequacious notes
er delicious surges sink and rise,
ch a soft floating witchery of sound
twilight Elfins make, when they at eve
yage on gentle gales from Fairy-land,

Where Melodies round honey-dropping flowers,
Footless and wild, like birds of Paradise,
Nor pause, nor perch, hovering on untamed wing!
O! the one life within us and abroad,
Which meets all motion and becomes its soul,
A light in sound, a sound-like power in light
Rhythm in all thought, and joyance every where—
Methinks, it should have been impossible
Not to love all things in a world so filled;
Where the breeze warbles, and the mute still air
Is Music slumbering on her instrument.

And thus, my love! as on the mid-way slope
Of yonder hill I stretch my limbs at noon,
Whilst through my half-closed eye-lids I behold
The sunbeams dance, like diamonds, on the main,
And tranquil muse upon tranquillity;
Full many a thought uncalled and undetained,
And many idle flitting phantasies,
Traverse my indolent and passive brain,
As wild and various as the random gales
That swell and flutter on this subject lute!

And what if all of animated nature
Be but organic harps diversely framed,
That tremble into thought, as o'er them sweeps
Plastic and vast, one intellectual breeze,
At once the Soul of each, and God of all?

But thy more serious eye a mild reproof
Darts, O beloved woman! nor such thoughts
Dim and unhallowed dost thou not reject,
And biddest me walk humbly with my God.
Meek daughter in the family of Christ!

Well hast thou said and holily dispraised
These shapings of the unregenerate mind;
Bubbles that glitter as they rise and break
On vain Philosophy's aye-babbling spring.
For never guiltless may I speak of him,
The Incomprehensible! save when with awe
I praise him, and with Faith that inly feels;
Who with his saving mercies healed me,
A sinful and most miserable man,
Wildered and dark, and gave me to possess
Peace, and this cot, and thee, dear honoured Maid!

1795.

A QUIET PLACE.

Low was our pretty Cot: our tallest rose
Peeped at the chamber-window. We could hear
At silent noon, and eve, and early morn,
The sea's faint murmur. In the open air
Our myrtles blossom'd; and across the porch
Thick jasmins twined: the little landscape round
Was green and woody, and refreshed the eye.
It was a spot which you might aptly call
The Valley of Seclusion!

*   *   *   *   *   *

                        Oft with patient ear
Long-listening to the viewless sky-lark's note
(Viewless, or haply for a moment seen
Gleaming on sunny wings) in whispered tones
I've said to my beloved, ' Such, sweet girl!

The inobtrusive song of Happiness,
Unearthly minstrelsy! then only heard
When the soul seeks to hear; when all is hushed,
And the heart listens!'

                    But the time, when first
From that low dell, steep up the stony mount
I climbed with perilous toil and reached the top,
Oh! what a goodly scene!   *Here* the bleak mount,
The bare bleak mountain speckled thin with sheep;
Grey clouds, that shadowing spot the sunny fields;
And river, now with bushy rocks o'erbrowed,
Now winding bright and full, with naked banks;
And seats, and lawns, the abbey and the wood,
And cots, and hamlets, and faint city-spire;
The Channel *there*, the Islands and white sails,
Dim coasts, and cloud-like hills, and shoreless Ocean—
It seem'd like Omnipresence!   God, methought,
Had built him there a Temple: the whole World
Seemed imaged in its vast circumference:
No *wish* profaned my overwhelmed heart.
Blest hour! It was a luxury,—to be!

                                        1795.

To the

Rev. GEORGE COLERIDGE

OF OTTERY ST. MARY, DEVON,

With some poems.

" Notus in fratres animi paterni."—Hor. *Carm.* lib. 1, 2.

A BLESSED lot hath he, who having passed
His youth and early manhood in the stir
And turmoil of the world, retreats at length,
With cares that move, not agitate the heart,
To the same dwelling where his father dwelt;
And haply views his tottering little ones
Embrace those aged knees and climb that lap
On which first kneeling his own infancy
Lisped its brief prayer. Such, O my earliest friend!
Thy lot, and such thy brothers too enjoy.
At distance did ye climb life's upland road,
Yet cheered and cheering: now fraternal love
Hath drawn you to one centre. Be your days
Holy, and blest and blessing may ye live!

To me the Eternal Wisdom hath dispensed
A different fortune and more different mind—
Me from the spot where first I sprang to light
Too soon transplanted, ere my soul had fixed
Its first domestic loves; and hence through life

Chasing chance-started friendships. A brief while
Some have preserved me from life's pelting ills;
But, like a tree with leaves of feeble stem,
If the clouds lasted, and a sudden breeze
Ruffled the boughs, they on my head at once
Dropped the collected shower; and some most false,
False and fair-foliaged as the Manchineel,
Have tempted me to slumber in their shade
E'en 'mid the storm; then breathing subtlest damps,
Mixed their own venom with the rain from heaven,
That I woke poisoned! But, all praise to Him
Who gives us all things, more have yielded me
Permanent shelter; and beside one friend,
Beneath the impervious covert of one oak,
I've raised a lowly shed, and know the names
Of Husband and of Father; not unhearing
Of that divine and nightly-whispering voice,
Which from my childhood to maturer years
Spake to me of predestinated wreaths,
Bright with no fading colours!

       Yet at times
My soul is sad, that I have roamed through life
Still most a stranger, most with naked heart
At mine own home and birthplace: chiefly then,
When I remember thee, my earliest friend!
Thee, who didst watch my boyhood and my youth;
Didst trace my wanderings with a father's eye;
And boding evil yet still hoping good,
Rebuked each fault, and over all my woes
Sorrowed in silence!   He who counts alone
The beatings of the solitary heart,
That Being knows, how I have loved thee ever,
Loved as a brother, as a son revered thee!
Oh! 'tis to me an ever new delight,

To talk of thee and thine: or when the blast
Of the shrill winter, rattling our rude sash,
Endears the cleanly hearth and social bowl;
Or when as now, on some delicious eve,
We in our sweet sequestered orchard-plot
Sit on the tree crooked earth-ward; whose old boughs,
That hang above us in an arborous roof,
Stirred by the faint gale of departing May,
Send their loose blossoms slanting o'er our heads!

Nor dost not *thou* sometimes recall these hours,
When with the joy of hope thou gavest thine ear
To my wild firstling-lays.   Since then my song
Hath sounded deeper notes, such as beseem
Or that sad wisdom folly leaves behind,
Or such as, tuned to these tumultuous times,
Cope with the tempest's swell!

             These various strains,
Which I have framed in many a various mood,
Accept, my Brother! and (for some perchance
Will strike discordant on thy milder mind)
If aught of error or intemperate truth
Should meet thine ear, think thou that riper age
Will calm it down, and let thy love forgive it!

    Nether-Stowey, Somerset,
      May 26th, 1797.

THIS LIME-TREE BOWER MY PRISON.

ADDRESSED TO CHARLES LAMB, OF THE INDIA HOUS
LONDON.

WELL, they are gone, and here must I remain,
This lime-tree bower my prison! I have lost
Beauties and feelings, such as would have been
Most sweet to my remembrance even when age
Had dimmed mine eyes to blindness! They, meanwhil
Friends, whom I never more may meet again,
On springy heath, along the hill-top edge,
Wander in gladness, and wind down, perchance,
To that still roaring dell, of which I told;
The roaring dell, o'erwooded, narrow, deep,
And only speckled by the mid-day sun;
Where its slim trunk the ash from rock to rock
Flings arching like a bridge;—that branchless ash,
Unsunned and damp, whose few poor yellow leaves
Ne'er tremble in the gale, yet tremble still,
Fanned by the water-fall! and there my friends
Behold the dark green file of long lank weeds,
That all at once (a most fantastic sight!)
Still nod and drip beneath the dripping edge
Of the blue clay-stone.

              Now, my friends emerge
Beneath the wide wide Heaven—and view again
The many-steepled tract magnificent
Of hilly fields and meadows. and the sea,

With some fair bark, perhaps, whose sails light up
The slip of smooth clear blue betwixt two Isles
Of purple shadow! Yes! they wander on
In gladness all; but thou, methinks, most glad,
My gentle-hearted Charles! for thou hast pined
And hungered after Nature, many a year,
In the great City pent, winning thy way
With sad yet patient soul, through evil and pain
And strange calamity! Ah! slowly sink
Behind the western ridge, thou glorious Sun!
Shine in the slant beams of the sinking orb,
Ye purple heath-flowers! richlier burn, ye clouds!
Live in the yellow light, ye distant groves!
And kindle, thou blue Ocean! So my Friend
Struck with deep joy may stand, as I have stood,
Silent with swimming sense; yea, gazing round
On the wide landscape, gaze till all doth seem
Less gross than bodily; and of such hues
As veil the Almighty Spirit, when yet he makes
Spirits perceive his presence.

                    A delight
Comes sudden on my heart, and I am glad
As I myself were there! Nor in this bower,
This little lime-tree bower, have I not marked
Much that has soothed me. Pale beneath the blaze
Hung the transparent foliage; and I watched
Some broad and sunny leaf, and loved to see
The shadow of the leaf and stem above,
Dappling its sunshine! And that walnut-tree
Was richly tinged, and a deep radiance lay
Full on the ancient ivy, which usurps
Those fronting elms, and now, with blackest mass
Makes their dark branches gleam a lighter hue
Through the late twilight; and though now the bat

Wheels silent by, and not a swallow twitters,
Yet still the solitary humble-bee
Sings in the bean-flower! Henceforth I shall know
That Nature ne'er deserts the wise and pure;
No plot so narrow, be but Nature there,
No waste so vacant, but may well employ
Each faculty of sense, and keep the heart
Awake to Love and Beauty! and sometimes
'Tis well to be bereft of promised good,
That we may lift the soul, and contemplate
With lively joy the joys we cannot share.
My gentle-hearted Charles! when the last rook
Beat its straight path along the dusky air
Homewards, I blest it! deeming, its black wing
(Now a dim speck, now vanishing in light)
Had cross'd the mighty orb's dilated glory,
While thou stood'st gazing; or when all was still,
Flew creeking o'er thy head, and had a charm
For thee, my gentle-hearted Charles, to whom
No sound is dissonant which tells of Life.

1797.

FROST AT MIDNIGHT.

The Frost performs its secret ministry,
Unhelped by any wind.   The owlet's cry
Came loud—and hark, again! loud as before.
The inmates of my cottage, all at rest,
Have left me to that solitude, which suits
Abstruser musings: save that at my side
My cradled infant slumbers peacefully.
'Tis calm indeed! so calm, that it disturbs
And vexes meditation with its strange
And extreme silentness.   Sea, hill, and wood,
This populous village! Sea, and hill, and wood,
With all the numberless goings-on of life,
Inaudible as dreams! the thin blue flame
Lies on my low-burnt fire, and quivers not;
Only that film, which fluttered on the grate,
Still flutters there, the sole unquiet thing.
Methinks, its motion in this hush of nature
Gives it dim sympathies with me who live,
Making it a companionable form,
Whose puny flaps and freaks the idling Spirit
By its own moods interprets, every where
Echo or mirror seeking of itself,
And makes a toy of Thought.

                    But O! how oft,
How oft, at school, with most believing mind,
Presageful, have I gazed upon the bars,

To watch that fluttering *stranger*! and as oft
With unclosed lids, already had I dreamt
Of my sweet birth-place, and the old church-tower,
Whose bells, the poor man's only music, rang
From morn to evening, all the hot Fair-day,
So sweetly, that they stirred and haunted me
With a wild pleasure, falling on mine ear
Most like articulate sounds of things to come!
So gazed I, till the soothing things I dreamt
Lulled me to sleep, and sleep prolonged my dreams!
And so I brooded all the following morn,
Awed by the stern preceptor's face, mine eye
Fixed with mock study on my swimming book:
Save if the door half opened, and I snatched
A hasty glance, and still my heart leaped up,
For still I hoped to see the *stranger's* face.
Townsman, or aunt, or sister more beloved,
My play-mate when we both were clothed alike!

  Dear Babe, that sleepest cradled by my side,
Whose gentle breathings, heard in this deep calm,
Fill up the interspersed vacancies
And momentary pauses of the thought!
My babe so beautiful! it thrills my heart
With tender gladness, thus to look at thee,
And think that thou shalt learn far other lore,
And in far other scenes!   For I was reared
In the great city, pent 'mid cloisters dim,
And saw nought lovely but the sky and stars.
But *thou*, my babe! shalt wander like a breeze
By lakes and sandy shores, beneath the crags
Of ancient mountain, and beneath the clouds,
Which image in their bulk both lakes and shores
And mountain crags: so shalt thou see and hear

The lovely shapes and sounds intelligible
Of that eternal language, which thy God
Utters, who from eternity doth teach
Himself in all, and all things in himself.
Great universal Teacher! he shall mould
Thy spirit, and by giving make it ask.

Therefore all seasons shall be sweet to thee,
Whether the summer clothe the general earth
With greenness, or the redbreast sit and sing
Betwixt the tufts of snow on the bare branch
Of mossy apple-tree, while the nigh thatch
Smokes in the sun-thaw; whether the eave-drops fall
Heard only in the trances of the blast,
Or if the secret ministry of frost
Shall hang them up in silent icicles,
Quietly shining to the quiet Moon.

February 1798.

FEARS IN SOLITUDE.

WRITTEN AT NETHER STOWEY IN APRIL 1798, DURING
THE ALARM OF AN INVASION.

A GREEN and silent spot, amid the hills,
A small and silent dell!   O'er stiller place
No singing sky-lark ever poised himself.
The hills are heathy, save that swelling slope,
Which hath a gay and gorgeous covering on,
All golden with the never-bloomless furze,
Which now blooms most profusely: but the dell,
Bathed by the mist, is fresh and delicate
As vernal corn-field, or the unripe flax,
When, through its half-transparent stalks, at eve,
The level sunshine glimmers with green light.
Oh! 'tis a quiet spirit-healing nook!
Which all, methinks, would love; but chiefly he,
The humble man, who, in his youthful years,
Knew just so much of folly, as had made
His early manhood more securely wise!
Here he might lie on fern or withered heath,
While from the singing lark (that sings unseen
The minstrelsy that solitude loves best),
And from the sun, and from the breezy air,
Sweet influences trembled o'er his frame;
And he, with many feelings, many thoughts,
Made up a meditative joy, and found
Religious meanings in the forms of nature!
And so, his senses gradually wrapt
In a half sleep, he dreams of better worlds,

And dreaming hears thee still, O singing lark;
That singest like an angel in the clouds!

My God! it is a melancholy thing
For such a man, who would full fain preserve
His soul in calmness, yet perforce must feel
For all his human brethren—O my God!
It weighs upon the heart, that he must think
What uproar and what strife may now be stirring
This way or that way o'er these silent hills—
Invasion, and the thunder and the shout,
And all the crash of onset; fear and rage,
And undetermined conflict—even now,
Even now, perchance, and in his native isle:
Carnage and groans beneath this blessed sun!

     *   *   *   *   *

O native Britain! O my Mother Isle!
How shouldst thou prove aught else but dear and holy
To me, who from thy lakes and mountain-hills,
Thy clouds, thy quiet dales, thy rocks and seas,
Have drunk in all my intellectual life,
All sweet sensations, all ennobling thoughts,
All adoration of the God in nature,
All lovely and all honourable things,
Whatever makes this mortal spirit feel
The joy and greatness of its future being?
There lives nor form nor feeling in my soul
Unborrowed from my country! O divine
And beauteous island! thou hast been my sole
And most magnificent temple, in the which
I walk with awe, and sing my stately songs,
Loving the God that made me!—

                        May my fears,
My filial fears, be vain! and may the vaunts

And menace of the vengeful enemy
Pass like the gust, that roared and died away
In the distant tree: which heard, and only heard
In this low dell, bow'd not the delicate grass.

But now the gentle dew-fall sends abroad
The fruit-like perfume of the golden furze:
The light has left the summit of the hill,
Though still a sunny gleam lies beautiful,
Aslant the ivied beacon. Now farewell,
Farewell, awhile, O soft and silent spot!
On the green sheep-track, up the heathy hill,
Homeward I wind my way; and lo! recalled
From bodings that have well-nigh wearied me,
I find myself upon the brow, and pause
Startled! And after lonely sojourning
In such a quiet and surrounded nook,
This burst of prospect, here the shadowy main,
Dim-tinted, there the mighty majesty
Of that huge amphitheatre of rich
And elmy fields, seems like society—
Conversing with the mind, and giving it
A livelier impulse and a dance of thought!
And now, beloved Stowey! I behold
Thy church-tower, and, methinks, the four huge elms
Clustering, which mark the mansion of my friends;
And close behind them, hidden from my view,
Is my own lowly cottage, where my babe
And my babe's mother dwell in peace! With light
And quickened footsteps thitherward I tend,
Remembering thee, O green and silent dell!
And grateful, that by nature's quietness
And solitary musings, all my heart
Is soften'd, and made worthy to indulge
Love, and the thoughts that yearn for human kind.

THE NIGHTINGALE.

A CONVERSATION POEM, WRITTEN IN APRIL 1798.

'o cloud, no relique of the sunken day
'istinguishes the West, no long thin slip
f sullen light, no obscure trembling hues.
'ome, we will rest on this old mossy bridge!
'ou see the glimmer of the stream beneath,
'ut hear no murmuring: it flows silently,
'er its soft bed of verdure. All is still,
  balmy night! and though the stars be dim,
'et us think upon the vernal showers
'hat gladden the green earth, and we shall find
  pleasure in the dimness of the stars.
'nd hark! the Nightingale begins its song,
'Most musical, most melancholy ' bird!
  melancholy bird? Oh! idle thought!
'1 Nature there is nothing melancholy.
'ut some night-wandering man whose heart was pierced
'ith the remembrance of a grievous wrong,
'r slow distemper, or neglected love,
'nd so, poor wretch! fill'd all things with himself,
'nd made all gentle sounds tell back the tale
'f his own sorrow) he, and such as he,
'irst named these notes a melancholy strain.
'nd many a poet echoes the conceit;
'oet who hath been building up the rhyme
'hen he had better far have stretched his limbs
'eside a brook in mossy forest-dell,

F 43

By sun or moon-light, to the influxes
Of shapes and sounds and shifting elements
Surrendering his whole spirit, of his song
And of his fame forgetful! so his fame
Should share in Nature's immortality,
A venerable thing! and so his song
Should make all Nature lovelier, and itself
Be loved like Nature!

My Friend, and thou, our Sister! we have learnt
A different lore: we may not thus profane
Nature's sweet voices, always full of love
And joyance! 'Tis the merry Nightingale
That crowds, and hurries, and precipitates
With fast thick warble his delicious notes,
As he were fearful that an April night
Would be too short for him to utter forth
His love-chant, and disburthen his full soul
Of all its music!

                    And I know a grove
Of large extent, hard by a castle huge,
Which the great lord inhabits not; and so
This grove is wild with tangling underwood,
And the trim walks are broken up, and grass,
Thin grass and king-cups grow within the paths.
But never elsewhere in one place I knew
So many nightingales; and far and near,
In wood and thicket, over the wide grove,
They answer and provoke each other's songs,
With skirmish and capricious passagings,
And murmurs musical and swift jug-jug,
And one low piping sound more sweet than all—
Stirring the air with such an harmony,

That should you close your eyes, you might almost
forget it was not day! On moonlight bushes,
Whose dewy leaflets are but half-disclosed,
You may perchance behold them on the twigs,
Their bright, bright eyes, their eyes both bright and full,
Glistening, while many a glow-worm in the shade
Lights up her love-torch.

      A most gentle Maid,
Who dwelleth in her hospitable home
Hard by the castle, and at latest eve
(Even like a Lady vowed and dedicate
To something more than Nature in the grove)
Glides through the pathways; she knows all their notes,
That gentle Maid! and oft, a moment's space,
What time the moon was lost behind a cloud,
Hath heard a pause of silence; till the moon
Emerging, hath awakened earth and sky
With one sensation, and those wakeful birds
Have all burst forth in choral minstrelsy,
As if some sudden gale had swept at once
A hundred airy harps! And she hath watched
Many a nightingale perch giddily
On blossomy twig still swinging from the breeze,
And to that motion tune his wanton song
Like tipsy joy that reels with tossing head.

Farewell, O Warbler! till to-morrow eve,
And you, my friends! farewell, a short farewell!
We have been loitering long and pleasantly,
And now for our dear homes.—That strain again!
Full fain it would delay me. My dear babe,
Who, capable of no articulate sound,
Mars all things with his imitative lisp,

How he would place his hand beside his ear,
His little hand, the small forefinger up,
And bid us listen! And I deem it wise
To make him Nature's play-mate. He knows well
The evening-star; and once, when he awoke
In most distressful mood (some inward pain
Had made up that strange thing, an infant's dream),
I hurried with him to our orchard-plot,
And he beheld the moon, and, hushed at once,
Suspends his sobs, and laughs most silently,
While his fair eyes, that swam with undropped tears,
Did glitter in the yellow moon-beam! Well!—
It is a father's tale: But if that Heaven
Should give me life, his childhood shall grow up
Familiar with these songs, that with the night
He may associate joy.—Once more, farewell,
Sweet Nightingale! once more, my friends! farewell.

LINES

WRITTEN IN THE ALBUM AT ELBINGERODE, IN THE
HARTZ FOREST.

I stood on Brocken's sovran height, and saw
Woods crowding upon woods, hills over hills,
A surging scene, and only limited
By the blue distance. Heavily my way
Downward I dragged through fir-groves evermore,
Where bright green moss heaves in sepulchral forms
Speckled with sunshine; and, but seldom heard,
The sweet bird's song became an hollow sound;
And the breeze, murmuring indivisibly,
Preserved its solemn murmur most distinct

From many a note of many a waterfall,
And the brook's chatter; 'mid whose islet-stones
The dingy kidling with its tinkling bell
Leaped frolicsome, or old romantic goat
Sat, his white beard slow waving. I moved on
In low and languid mood: for I had found
That outward forms, the loftiest, still receive
Their finer influence from the Life within;—
Fair cyphers else: fair, but of import vague
Or unconcerning, where the heart not finds
History or prophecy of friend, or child,
Or gentle maid, our first and early love,
Or father, or the venerable name
Of our adored country! O thou Queen,
Thou delegated Deity of Earth,
O dear, dear England! how my longing eye
Turned westward, shaping in the steady clouds
Thy sands and high white cliffs!

                              My native Land!
Filled with the thought of thee this heart was proud,
Yea, mine eye swam with tears: that all the view
From sovran Brocken, woods and woody hills,
Floated away, like a departing dream,
Feeble and dim! Stranger, these impulses
Blame thou not lightly; nor will I profane,
With hasty judgment or injurious doubt,
That man's sublimer spirit, who can feel
That God is everywhere! the God who framed
Mankind to be one mighty family,
Himself our Father, and the World our Home.

                                   May 17, 1799.

CONSTANCY TO AN IDEAL OBJECT.

SINCE all that beat about in Nature's range,
Or veer or vanish; why should'st thou remain
The only constant in a world of change,
O yearning Thought! that liv'st but in the brain?
Call to the Hours, that in the distance play,
The faery people of the future day—
Fond Thought! not one of all that shining swarm
Will breathe on *thee* with life-enkindling breath,
Till when, like strangers shelt'ring from a storm,
Hope and Despair meet in the porch of Death!
Yet still thou haunt'st me; and though well I see,
She is not thou, and only thou art she,
Still, still as though some dear *embodied* Good,
Some *living* Love before my eyes there stood
With answering look a ready ear to lend,
I mourn to thee and say—'Ah! loveliest friend!
That this the meed of all my toils might be,
To have a home, an English home, and thee!'
Vain repetition!   Home and Thou are one.
The peacefullest cot, the moon shall shine upon,
Lulled by the thrush and wakened by the lark,
Without thee were but a becalmed bark,
Whose helmsman on an ocean waste and wide
Sits mute and pale his mouldering helm beside.

And art thou nothing? Such thou art, as when
The woodman winding westward up the glen

At wintry dawn, where o'er the sheep-track's maze
The viewless snow-mist weaves a glist'ning haze,
Sees full before him, gliding without tread,
An image with a glory round its head;
The enamoured rustic worships its fair hues,
Nor knows he *makes* the shadow he pursues!

? 1805.

THE GARDEN OF BOCCACCIO.

Of late, in one of those most weary hours,
When life seems emptied of all genial powers,
A dreary mood, which he who ne'er has known
May bless his happy lot, I sate alone;
And, from the numbing spell to win relief,
Call'd on the Past for thought of glee or grief.
In vain! bereft alike of grief and glee,
I sate and cow'r'd o'er my own vacancy!
And as I watch'd the dull continuous ache,
Which, all else slumb'ring, seem'd alone to wake;
O Friend! long wont to notice, yet conceal,
And soothe by silence what words cannot heal,
I but half saw that quiet hand of thine
Place on my desk this exquisite design.
Boccaccio's Garden and its faery,
The love, the joyaunce, and the gallantry!
An Idyll, with Boccaccio's spirit warm,
Framed in the silent poesy of form.
Like flocks adown a newly-bathed steep
   Emerging from a mist: or like a stream
Of music soft that not dispels the sleep,
   But casts in happier moulds the slumberer's dream,

Gazed by an idle eye with silent might
The picture stole upon my inward sight.
A tremulous warmth crept gradual o'er my chest,
As though an infant's finger touch'd my breast.
And one by one (I know not whence) were brought
All spirits of power that most had stirr'd my thought
In selfless boyhood, on a new world tost
Of wonder, and in its own fancies lost;
Or charm'd my youth, that, kindled from above,
Loved ere it loved, and sought a form for love;
Or lent a lustre to the earnest scan
Of manhood, musing what and whence is man!
Wild strain of Scalds, that in the sea-worn caves
Rehearsed their war-spell to the winds and waves;
Or fateful hymn of those prophetic maids,
That call'd on Hertha in deep forest glades;
Or minstrel lay, that cheer'd the baron's feast;
Or rhyme of city pomp, of monk and priest,
Judge, mayor, and many a guild in long array,
To high-church pacing on the great saint's day.
And many a verse which to myself I sang,
That woke the tear yet stole away the pang,
Of hopes which in lamenting I renew'd.
And last, a matron now, of sober mien,
Yet radiant still and with no earthly sheen,
Whom as a faery child my childhood woo'd
Even in my dawn of thought—Philosophy;
Though then unconscious of herself, pardie,
She bore no other name than Poesy;
And, like a gift from heaven, in lifeful glee,
That had but newly left a mother's knee,
Prattled and play'd with bird and flower, and stone,
As if with elfin playfellows well known,
And life reveal'd to innocence alone.

Thanks, gentle artist! now I can descry
Thy fair creation with a mastering eye,
And *all* awake! And now in fix'd gaze stand,
Now wander through the Eden of thy hand;
Praise the green arches, on the fountain clear
See fragment shadows of the crossing deer;
And with that serviceable nymph I stoop
The crystal from its restless pool to scoop.
I see no longer! I myself am there,
Sit on the ground-sward, and the banquet share.
'Tis I, that sweep that lute's love-echoing strings,
And gaze upon the maid who gazing sings;
Or pause and listen to the tinkling bells
From the high tower, and think that there she dwells.
With old Boccaccio's soul I stand possest,
And breathe an air like life, that swells my chest.

The brightness of the world, O thou once free,
And always fair, rare land of courtesy!
O Florence! with the Tuscan fields and hills
And famous Arno, fed with all their rills;
Thou brightest star of star-bright Italy!
Rich, ornate, populous, all treasures thine,
The golden corn, the olive, and the vine.
Fair cities, gallant mansions, castles old,
And forests, where beside his leafy hold
The sullen boar hath heard the distant horn,
And whets his tusks against the gnarled thorn;
Palladian palace with its storied halls;
Fountains, where Love lies listening to their falls;
Gardens, where flings the bridge its airy span,
And Nature makes her happy home with man;
Where many a gorgeous flower is duly fed
With its own rill, on its own spangled bed,
And wreathes the marble urn, or leans its head,

A mimic mourner, that with veil withdrawn
Weeps liquid gems, the presents of the dawn;—
Thine all delights, and every muse is thine;
And more than all, the embrace and intertwine
Of all with all in gay and twinkling dance!
'Mid gods of Greece and warriors of romance.
See! Boccace sits, unfolding on his knees
The new-found roll of old Mæonides;
But from his mantle's fold, and near the heart,
Peers Ovid's Holy Book of Love's sweet smart! [1]
O all-enjoying and all-blending sage,
Long be it mine to con thy mazy page,
Where, half conceal'd, the eye of fancy views
Fauns, nymphs, and winged saints, all gracious to
        thy muse!

Still in thy garden let me watch their pranks,
And see in Dian's vest between the ranks
Of the trim vines, some maid that half believes
The *vestal* fires, of which her lover grieves,
With that sly satyr peeping through the leaves!

                                        1828.

[1] I know few more striking or more interesting proofs of the
overwhelming influence which the study of the Greek and
Roman classics exercised on the judgments, feelings, and
imaginations of the literati of Europe at the commencement
of the restoration of literature, than the passage in the Filo-
copo of Boccaccio: where the sage instructor, Racheo, as soon
as the young prince and the beautiful girl Biancofiore had
learned their letters, sets them to study the Holy Book, Ovid's
Art of Love. " Incominciò Racheo a mettere il suo officio
in esecuzione con intera sollecitudine. E loro, in breve tempo,
insegnato a conoscer le lettere, fece leggere il santo libro
d'Ovvidio, nel quale il sommo poeta mostra, come i santi
fuochi di Venere si debbano ne freddi cuori accendere."

II.

ODES AND HYMNS

ODE ON THE DEPARTING YEAR.

Ἰοὺ ἰού, ὦ ὦ κακά.

'Ὑπ' αὖ με δεινὸς ὀρθομαντείας πόνος
Στροβεῖ, ταράσσων φροιμίοις ἐφημίοις

.   .   .   .

Τὸ μέλλον ἥξει. Καὶ σύ μ' ἐν τάχει παρὼν
Ἄγαν ἀληθόμαντιν οἰκτείρας ἐρεῖς.

Æschyl, Agam. 1215–18; 1240–41.

ARGUMENT.—The Ode commences with an address to the Divine Providence, that regulates into one vast harmony all the events of time, however calamitous some of them may appear to mortals. The second Strophe calls on men to suspend their private joys and sorrows, and devote them for a while to the cause of human nature in general. The first Epode speaks of the Empress of Russia, who died of an apoplexy on the 17th of November 1796; having just concluded a subsidiary treaty with the Kings combined against France. The first and second Antistrophe describe the Image of the Departing Year, etc., as in a vision. The second Epode prophesies, in anguish of spirit, the downfall of this country.

I.

SPIRIT who sweepest the wild harp of Time!
  It is most hard, with an untroubled ear
  Thy dark inwoven harmonies to hear!
Yet, mine eye fixed on Heaven's unchanging clime
Long had I listened, free from mortal fear,
  With inward stillness, and submitted mind;
  When lo! its folds far waving on the wind,
I saw the train of the Departing Year!
  Starting from my silent sadness
  Then with no unholy madness
Ere yet the entered cloud foreclosed my sight,
I raised the impetuous song, and solemnized his flight.

II.

Hither, from the recent tomb,
From the prison's direr gloom,
From distemper's midnight anguish;
And thence, where poverty doth waste and languish;
Or where, his two bright torches blending,
Love illumines Manhood's maze;
Or where o'er cradled infants blending,
Hope has fixed her wistful gaze;
Hither, in perplexed dance,
Ye woes! ye young-eyed Joys! advance!
By Time's wild harp, and by the hand
Whose indefatigable sweep
Raises its fateful strings from sleep,
I bid you haste, a mixed tumultuous band!
From every private bower,
And each domestic hearth,
Haste for one solemn hour;
And with a loud and yet a louder voice,
O'er Nature struggling in portentous birth,
Weep and rejoice!
Still echoes the dread Name that o'er the earth
Let slip the storm, and woke the brood of hell:
And now advance in saintly jubilee
Justice and Truth!   They too have heard thy spell,
They too obey thy name, divinest Liberty!

III.

I marked Ambition in his war-array!
I heard the mailed Monarch's troublous cry—
'Ah! wherefore does the Northern Conqueress stay!
Groans not her chariot on its onward way?'
Fly, mailed Monarch, fly!

Stunned by Death's twice mortal mace,
No more on Murder's lurid face
The insatiate hag shall gloat with drunken eye!
Manes of the unnumbered slain!
Ye that gasped on Warsaw's plain!
Ye that erst at Ismail's tower,
When human ruin choked the streams,
Fell in conquest's glutted hour,
'Mid women's shrieks and infants' screams!
Spirits of the uncoffined slain,
Sudden blasts of triumph swelling,
Oft, at night, in misty train,
Rush around her narrow dwelling!
The exterminating fiend is fled—
(Foul her life, and dark her doom)
Mighty armies of the dead
Dance, like death-fires, round her tomb!
Then with prophetic song relate,
Each some tyrant-murderer's fate!

IV.

Departing Year! 'twas on no earthly shore
My soul beheld thy vision! Where alone,
Voiceless and stern, before the cloudy throne,
Aye Memory sits: thy robe inscribed with gore,
With many an unimaginable groan
Thou storied'st thy sad hours! Silence ensued,
Deep silence o'er the ethereal multitude,
Whose locks with wreaths, whose wreaths with
    glories shone.
Then, his eye wild ardours glancing,
From the choired gods advancing,
The Spirit of the Earth made reverence meet,
And stood up, beautiful, before the cloudy seat.

v.

Throughout the blissful throng,
  Hushed were harp and song:
Till wheeling round the throne the Lampads seven,
  (The mystic Words of Heaven)
  Permissive signal make:
The fervent Spirit bowed, then spread his wings and
      spake!
' Thou in stormy blackness throning
  Love and uncreated Light,
By the Earth's unsolaced groaning,
  Seize thy terrors, Arm of might!
By Peace with proffer'd insult scared,
  Masked hate and envying scorn!
  By years of havoc yet unborn!
And Hunger's bosom to the frost-winds bared!
  But chief by Afric's wrongs,
    Strange, horrible, and foul!
  By what deep guilt belongs
To the deaf Synod, ' full of gifts and lies!'
By Wealth's insensate laugh! by Torture's howl!
      Avenger, rise!
For ever shall the thankless Island scowl,
  Her quiver full, and with unbroken bow?
Speak! from thy storm-black Heaven O speak aloud!
      And on the darkling foe
Open thine eye of fire from some uncertain cloud!
  O dart the flash! O rise and deal the blow!
The Past to thee, to thee the Future cries!
  Hark! how wide Nature joins her groans below!
    Rise, God of Nature! rise.'

vi.

The voice had ceased, the vision fled;
Yet still I gasped and reeled with dread.

And ever, when the dream of night
Renews the phantom to my sight,
Cold sweat-drops gather on my limbs;
   My ears throb hot; my eye-balls start;
My brain with horrid tumult swims;
   Wild is the tempest of my heart;
And my thick and struggling breath
Imitates the toil of death!
No stranger agony confounds
   The soldier on the war-field spread,
When all foredone with toil and wounds,
   Death-like he dozes among heaps of dead!
(The strife is o'er, the day-light fled,
   And the night-wind clamours hoarse!
See! the starting wretch's head
   Lies pillowed on a brother's corse!)

VII.

Not yet enslaved, not wholly vile,
O Albion! O my mother Isle!
Thy valleys, fair as Eden's bowers,
Glitter green with sunny showers;
Thy grassy uplands' gentle swells
   Echo to the bleat of flocks;
(Those grassy hills, those glittering dells
   Proudly ramparted with rocks)
And Ocean mid his uproar wild
Speaks safety to his Island-child!
   Hence for many a fearless age
   Has social Quiet loved thy shore;
   Nor ever proud invader's rage
Or sacked thy towers, or stained thy fields with gore.

VIII.

Abandon'd of Heaven! mad Avarice thy guide,
At cowardly distance, yet kindling with pride—
'Mid thy herds and thy corn-fields secure thou hast stoo
And join'd the wild yelling of Famine and Blood!
The nations curse thee! They with eager wondering
 Shall hear Destruction, like a vulture, scream!
 Strange-eyed Destruction! who with many a dream
Of central fires through nether seas upthundering
 Soothes her fierce solitude; yet as she lies
 By livid fount, or red volcanic stream,
 If ever to her lidless dragon-eyes,
 O Albion! thy predestined ruins rise,
The fiend-hag on her perilous couch doth leap,
Muttering distempered triumph in her charmed sleep.

IX.

 Away, my soul, away!
 In vain, in vain the birds of warning sing—
And hark! I hear the famished brood of prey
Flap their lank pennons on the groaning wind!
 Away, my soul, away!
 I unpartaking of the evil thing,
  With daily prayer and daily toil
  Soliciting for food my scanty soil,
 Have wailed my country with a loud Lament.
Now I recentre my immortal mind
 In the deep sabbath of meek self-content;
Cleansed from the vaporous passions that bedim
God's Image, sister of the Seraphim.

FRANCE: AN ODE.

I.

Ye Clouds! that far above me float and pause,
  Whose pathless march no mortal may controul!
  Ye Ocean-Waves! that, whereso'er ye roll,
Yield homage only to eternal laws!
Ye Woods! that listen to the night-birds' singing,
  Midway the smooth and perilous slope reclined,
Save when your own imperious branches swinging,
  Have made a solemn music of the wind!
Where, like a man beloved of God,
Through glooms, which never woodman trod,
    How oft, pursuing fancies holy,
My moonlight way o'er flowering weeds I wound,
    Inspired, beyond the guess of folly,
By each rude shape and wild unconquerable sound!
O ye loud Waves! and O ye Forests high!
  And O ye Clouds that far above me soared!
Thou rising Sun! thou blue rejoicing Sky!
  Yea, every thing that is and will be free!
  Bear witness for me, whereso'er ye be,
  With what deep worship I have still adored
    The spirit of divinest Liberty.

II.

When France in wrath her giant-limbs upreared,
  And with that oath, which smote air, earth, and sea,
  Stamped her strong foot and said she would be free,
Bear witness for me, how I hoped and feared!

With what a joy my lofty gratulation
   Unawed I sang, amid a slavish band:
And when to whelm the disenchanted nation,
   Like fiends embattled by a wizard's wand,
     The Monarchs marched in evil day,
     And Britain join'd the dire array;
   Though dear her shores and circling ocean,
Though many friendships, many youthful loves
   Had swoln the patriot emotion
And flung a magic light o'er all her hills and groves;
Yet still my voice, unaltered, sang defeat
   To all that braved the tyrant-quelling lance,
And shame too long delay'd and vain retreat!
For ne'er, O Liberty! with partial aim
I dimmed thy light or damped thy holy flame;
   But blessed the pæans of delivered France,
And hung my head and wept at Britain's name.

III.

'And what,' I said, 'though Blasphemy's loud scream
   With that sweet music of deliverance strove!
   Though all the fierce and drunken passions wove
A dance more wild than e'er was maniac's dream!
   Ye storms, that round the dawning east assembled,
The Sun was rising, though ye hid his light!'
   And when, to soothe my soul, that hoped and
     trembled,
The dissonance ceased, and all seemed calm and bright
   When France her front deep-warr'd and gory
   Concealed with clustering wreaths of glory;
     When, insupportably advancing,
   Her arm made mockery of the warrior's ramp;
     While timid looks of fury glancing,
   Domestic treason, crushed beneath her fatal stamp

Writhed like a wounded dragon in his gore;
  Then I reproached my fears that would not flee;
'And soon,' I said, 'shall Wisdom teach her lore
In the low huts of them that toil and groan!
And, conquering by her happiness alone,
  Shall France compel the nations to be free,
Till Love and Joy look round, and call the Earth
    their own.'

IV.

Forgive me, Freedom! O forgive those dreams!
  I hear thy voice, I hear thy loud lament,
  From bleak Helvetia's icy caverns sent—
I hear thy groans upon her blood-stained streams!
  Heroes, that for your peaceful country perished,
And ye that, fleeing, spot your mountain-snows
  With bleeding wounds; forgive me, that I
    cherished
One thought that ever blessed your cruel foes!
  To scatter rage and traitorous guilt
  Where Peace her jealous home had built;
    A patriot-race to disinherit
Of all that made their stormy wilds so dear;
    And with inexpiable spirit
To taint the bloodless freedom of the mountaineer—
O France, that mockest Heaven, adulterous, blind,
  And patriot only in pernicious toils!
Are these thy boasts, Champion of human kind?
  To mix with Kings in the low lust of sway,
Yell in the hunt, and share the murderous prey;
To insult the shrine of Liberty with spoils
  From freemen torn; to tempt and to betray?

v.

The Sensual and the Dark rebel in vain,
  Slaves by their own compulsion!   In mad game
They burst their manacles and wear the name
  Of Freedom, graven on a heavier chain!
O Liberty! with profitless endeavour
Have I pursued thee, many a weary hour;
  But thou nor swell'st the victor's strain, nor ever
Didst breathe thy soul in forms of human power.
  Alike from all, howe'er they praise thee,
    (Nor prayer, nor boastful name delays thee)
    Alike from Priestcraft's harpy minions,
  And factious Blasphemy's obscener slaves,
    Thou speedest on thy subtle pinions,
The guide of homeless winds, and playmate of the
    waves!
And there I felt thee!—on that sea-cliff's verge,
  Whose pines, scarce travelled by the breeze above,
Had made one murmur with the distant surge!
Yes, while I stood and gazed, my temples bare,
And shot my being through earth, sea and air,
  Possessing all things with intensest love,
    O Liberty! my spirit felt thee there.
                  February 1798.

DEJECTION: AN ODE.

WRITTEN APRIL 4, 1802.

> Late, late yestreen I saw the new Moon,
> With the old Moon in her arms;
> And I fear, I fear, my Master dear!
> We shall have a deadly storm.
> *Ballad of Sir Patrick Spence.*

I.

ELL! If the Bard was weather-wise, who made
The grand old ballad of Sir Patrick Spence,
This night, so tranquil now, will not go hence
nroused by winds, that ply a busier trade
nan those which mould yon cloud in lazy flakes,
r the dull sobbing draft, that moans and rakes
    Upon the strings of this Æolian lute,
    Which better far were mute.
For lo! the New-moon winter-bright!
And overspread with phantom light,
  (With swimming phantom light o'erspread
  But rimmed and circled by a silver thread)
see the old Moon in her lap, foretelling
The coming-on of rain and squally blast.
nd oh! that even now the gust were swelling,
  And the slant night-shower driving loud and fast!
nose sounds which oft have raised me, whilst they awed,
    And sent my soul abroad,
ight now perhaps their wonted impulse give,
ight startle this dull pain, and make it move and live!

II.

A grief without a pang, void, dark, and drear,
    A stifled, drowsy, unimpassioned grief,
    Which finds no natural outlet, no relief,
        In word, or sigh, or tear—
O Lady! in this wan and heartless mood,
To other thoughts by yonder throstle woo'd,
    All this long eve, so balmy and serene,
Have I been gazing on the western sky,
    And its peculiar tint of yellow green:
And still I gaze—and with how blank an eye!
And those thin clouds above, in flakes and bars,
That give away their motion to the stars;
Those stars, that glide behind them or between,
Now sparkling, now bedimmed, but always seen:
Yon crescent Moon, as fixed as if it grew
In its own cloudless, starless lake of blue;
I see them all so excellently fair,
I see, not feel, how beautiful they are!

III.

    My genial spirits fail;
    And what can these avail
To lift the smothering weight from off my breast?
    It were a vain endeavour,
    Though I should gaze for ever
On that green light that lingers in the west:
I may not hope from outward forms to win
The passion and the life, whose fountains are within.

IV.

O Lady! we receive but what we give,
And in our life alone does Nature live:

Ours is her wedding-garment, ours her shroud!
   And would we aught behold, of higher worth,
Than that inanimate cold world allowed
To the poor loveless ever-anxious crowd,
   Ah! from the soul itself must issue forth
A light, a glory, a fair luminous cloud
      Enveloping the Earth—
And from the soul itself must there be sent
   A sweet and potent voice, of its own birth,
Of all sweet sounds the life and element!

v.

O pure of heart! thou need'st not ask of me
What this strong music in the soul may be!
What, and wherein it doth exist,
This light, this glory, this fair luminous mist,
This beautiful and beauty-making power.
   Joy, virtuous Lady! Joy that ne'er was given,
Save to the pure, and in their purest hour,
Life, and Life's effluence, cloud at once and shower,
Joy, Lady! is the spirit and the power,
Which wedding Nature to us gives in dower,
   A new Earth and new Heaven,
Undreamt of by the sensual and the proud—
Joy is the sweet voice, Joy the luminous cloud—
      We in ourselves rejoice!
And thence flows all that charms or ear or sight,
   All melodies the echoes of that voice,
All colours a suffusion from that light.

vi.

There was a time when, though my path was rough,
   This joy within me dallied with distress,
And all misfortunes were but as the stuff
   Whence Fancy made me dreams of happiness:

For Hope grew round me, like the twining vine,
And fruits, and foliage, not my own, seemed mine.
But now afflictions bow me down to earth:
Nor care I that they rob me of my mirth;
　　But oh! each visitation
Suspends what nature gave me at my birth,
　My shaping spirit of Imagination.
For not to think of what I needs must feel,
　But to be still and patient, all I can;
And haply by abstruse research to steal
　From my own nature all the natural man—
　This was my sole resource, my only plan:
Till that which suits a part infects the whole,
And now is almost grown the habit of my soul.

VII.

Hence, viper thoughts, that coil around my mind,
　　Reality's dark dream!
I turn from you, and listen to the wind,
　Which long has raved unnoticed.
　　　What a scream
Of agony by torture lengthened out
That lute sent forth! Thou Wind, that rav'st witho
　Bare crag, or mountain-tairn, or blasted tree,
Or pine-grove whither woodman never clomb,
Or lonely house, long held the witches' home,
　Methinks were fitter instruments for thee,
Mad Lutanist! who in this month of showers,
Of dark-brown gardens, and of peeping flowers,
Mak'st Devil's yule, with worse than wintry song,
The blossoms, buds, and timorous leaves among.
　Thou actor, perfect in all tragic sounds!
Thou mighty Poet, even to frenzy bold!

What tell'st thou now about?
'Tis of the rushing of an host in rout,
With groans of trampled men, with smarting
    wounds—
At once they groan with pain, and shudder with the
    cold!
But hush! there is a pause of deepest silence!
And all that noise, as of a rushing crowd,
With groans, and tremulous shudderings—all is over—
It tells another tale, with sounds less deep and loud!
    A tale of less affright,
    And tempered with delight,
As Otway's self had framed the tender lay,
    'Tis of a little child
    Upon a lonesome wild,
Not far from home, but she hath lost her way:
And now moans low in bitter grief and fear,
And now screams loud, and hopes to make her
    mother hear.

VIII.

'Tis midnight, but small thoughts have I of sleep:
Full seldom may my friend such vigils keep!
Visit her, gentle Sleep! with wings of healing,
    And may this storm be but a mountain-birth,
May all the stars hang bright above her dwelling,
    Silent as though they watched the sleeping Earth!
        With light heart may she rise,
        Gay fancy, cheerful eyes,
    Joy lift her spirit, joy attune her voice;
To her may all things live, from pole to pole,
Their life the eddying of her living soul!
    O simple spirit, guided from above,
Dear Lady! friend devoutest of my choice,
Thus mayest thou ever, evermore rejoice.

ODE TO TRANQUILLITY.

TRANQUILLITY! thou better name
Than all the family of Fame!
Thou ne'er wilt leave my riper age
To low intrigue, or factious rage;
For oh! dear child of thoughtful Truth,
To thee I gave my early youth,
And left the bark, and blest the steadfast shore,
Ere yet the tempest rose and scared me with its roar.

Who late and lingering seeks thy shrine,
On him but seldom, Power divine,
Thy spirit rests! Satiety
And Sloth, poor counterfeits of thee,
Mock the tired worldling. Idle Hope
And dire Remembrance interlope,
To vex the feverish slumbers of the mind:
The bubble floats before, the spectre stalks behind.

But me thy gentle hand will lead
At morning through the accustomed mead;
And in the sultry summer's heat
Will build me up a mossy seat;
And when the gust of Autumn crowds,
And breaks the busy moonlight clouds,
Thou best the thought canst raise, the heart attune,
Light as the busy clouds, calm as the gliding moon.

The feeling heart, the searching soul,
To thee I dedicate the whole!
And while within myself I trace
The greatness of some future race,
Aloof with hermit-eye I scan
The present works of present man—
A wild and dream-like trade of blood and guile,
Too foolish for a tear, too wicked for a smile!

1801.

HYMN TO THE EARTH.

[IMITATED FROM STOLBERG'S *HYMNE AN DIE ERDE.*]

HEXAMETERS.

EARTH! thou mother of numberless children, the
    nurse and the mother,
Hail! O Goddess, thrice hail! Blest be thou! and,
    blessing, I hymn thee!
Forth, ye sweet sounds! from my harp, and my
    voice shall float on your surges--
Soar thou aloft, O my soul! and bear up my song
    on thy pinions.

Travelling the vale with mine eyes—green meadows
    and lake with green island,
Dark in its basin of rock, and the bare stream flowing
    in brightness,
Thrill'd with thy beauty and love in the wooded
    slope of the mountain,
Here, great mother, I lie, thy child, with his head on
    thy bosom!

Playful the spirits of noon, that rushing soft through
    thy tresses,
Green-hair'd goddess! refresh me; and hark! as they
    hurry or linger,
Fill the pause of my harp, or sustain it with musical
    murmurs.
Into my being thou murmurest joy, and tenderest
    sadness
Shedd'st thou, like dew, on my heart, till the joy and
    the heavenly sadness
Pour themselves forth from my heart in tears, and
    the hymn of thanksgiving.

Earth! thou mother of numberless children, the
    nurse and the mother,
Sister thou of the stars, and beloved by the Sun, the
    rejoicer!
Guardian and friend of the moon, O Earth, whom the
    comets forget not,
Yea, in the measureless distance wheel round and
    again they behold thee!
Fadeless and young (and what if the latest birth of
    creation?)
Bride and consort of Heaven, that looks down upon
    thee enamour'd!
Say, mysterious Earth! O say, great mother and
    goddess,
Was it not well with thee then, when first thy lap was
    ungirdled,
Thy lap to the genial Heaven, the day that he woo'd
    thee and won thee!

Fair was thy blush, the fairest and first of the blushes
    of morning!
Deep was the shudder, O Earth! the throe of thy
    self-retention:

Inly thou strovest to flee, and didst seek thyself at
    thy centre!

Mightier far was the joy of thy sudden resilience;
    and forthwith

Myriad myriads of lives teem'd forth from the
    mighty embracement.

Thousand-fold tribes of dwellers, impell'd by
    thousand-fold instincts,

Fill'd, as a dream, the wide waters; the rivers sang
    on their channels;

Laugh'd on their shores the hoarse seas; the yearn-
    ing ocean swell'd upward;

Young life low'd through the meadows, the woods,
    and the echoing mountains,

Wander'd bleating in valleys, and warbled on
    blossoming branches.

    •   •   •   •   •   •

                        ? 1799.

ON A CATARACT

FROM A CAVERN NEAR THE SUMMIT OF A MOUNTAIN PRECIPICE.

[AFTER STOLBERG'S *UNSTERBLICHER JÜNGLING.*]

STROPHE.

UNPERISHING youth!
Thou leapest from forth
The cell of thy hidden nativity;
Never mortal saw
The cradle of the strong one;
Never mortal heard
The gathering of his voices;
The deep-murmur'd charm of the son of the rock,
That is lisp'd evermore at his slumberless fountain.
There's a cloud at the portal, a spray-woven veil
At the shrine of his ceaseless renewing;
It embosoms the roses of dawn,
It entangles the shafts of the noon,
And into the bed of its stillness
The moonshine sinks down as in slumber,
That the son of the rock, that the nursling of heaven
May be born in a holy twilight!

1799.

THE VISIT OF THE GODS.

IMITATED FROM SCHILLER.

NEVER, believe me,
  Appear the Immortals,
   Never alone:
Scarce had I welcomed the Sorrow-beguiler,
Iacchus! but in came Boy Cupid the Smiler;
Lo! Phœbus the Glorious descends from his throne!
They advance, they float in, the Olympians all!
   With Divinities fills my
    Terrestrial hall!

   How shall I yield you
   Due entertainment,
    Celestial quire?
Me rather, bright guests! with your wings of
  upbuoyance
Bear aloft to your homes, to your banquets of joyance,
That the roofs of Olympus may echo my lyre!
Hah! we mount! on their pinions they waft up my
  soul!
   O give me the nectar!
   O fill me the bowl!

   Give him the nectar!
   Pour out for the poet,
    Hebe! pour free!
Quicken his eyes with celestial dew,
That Styx the detested no more he may view,
And like one of us Gods may conceit him to be!
Thanks, Hebe! I quaff it! Io Pæan, I cry!
   The wine of the Immortals
    Forbids me to die!   *1799.*

HYMN BEFORE SUN-RISE IN THE
VALE OF CHAMOUNI.

Besides the Rivers, Arve and Arveiron, which have their
sources in the foot of Mont Blanc, five conspicuous torrents
rush down its sides; and within a few paces of the Glaciers,
the Gentiana Major grows in immense numbers, with its
" flowers of loveliest blue."

HAST thou a charm to stay the morning-star
In his steep course? So long he seems to pause
On thy bald awful head, O sovran BLANC!
The Arve and Arveiron at thy base
Rave ceaselessly; but thou, most awful Form!
Risest from forth thy silent sea of pines,
How silently! Around thee and above
Deep is the air and dark, substantial, black,
An ebon mass: methinks thou piercest it,
As with a wedge! But when I look again,
It is thine own calm home, thy crystal shrine,
Thy habitation from eternity!
O dread and silent Mount! I gazed upon thee,
Till thou, still present to the bodily sense,
Didst vanish from my thought: entranced in prayer
I worshipped the Invisible alone.

Yet, like some sweet beguiling melody,
So sweet, we know not we are listening to it,
Thou, the meanwhile, wast blending with my Though
Yea, with my Life and Life's own secret joy:
Till the dilating Soul, enrapt, transfused,
Into the mighty vision passing—there
As in her natural form, swelled vast to Heaven!

Awake, my soul! not only passive praise
Thou owest! not alone these swelling tears,
Mute thanks and secret ecstasy! Awake,
Voice of sweet song! Awake, my heart, awake!
Green vales and icy cliffs, all join my hymn.

Thou first and chief, sole sovereign of the Vale!
O struggling with the darkness all the night,
And visited all night by troops of stars,
Or when they climb the sky or when they sink:
Companion of the morning-star at dawn,
Thyself Earth's rosy star, and of the dawn
Co-herald: wake, O wake, and utter praise!
Who sank thy sunless pillars deep in Earth?
Who fill'd thy countenance with rosy light?
Who made thee parent of perpetual streams?

And you, ye five wild torrents fiercely glad!
Who called you forth from night and utter death,
From dark and icy caverns called you forth,
Down those precipitous, black, jagged rocks,
For ever shattered and the same for ever?
Who gave you your invulnerable life,
Your strength, your speed, your fury, and your joy,
Unceasing thunder and eternal foam?
And who commanded (and the silence came),
Here let the billows stiffen, and have rest?

Ye Ice-falls! ye that from the mountain's brow
Adown enormous ravines slope amain—
Torrents, methinks, that heard a mighty voice,
And stopped at once amid their maddest plunge!
Motionless torrents! silent cataracts!
Who made you glorious as the Gates of Heaven
Beneath the keen full moon? Who bade the sun

Clothe you with rainbows? Who, with living flowe
Of loveliest blue, spread garlands at your feet?—
GOD! let the torrents, like a shout of nations,
Answer! and let the ice-plains echo, GOD!
GOD! sing ye meadow-streams with gladsome voice!
Ye pine-groves, with your soft and soul-like sounds
And they too have a voice, yon piles of snow,
And in their perilous fall shall thunder, GOD!

Ye living flowers that skirt the eternal frost!
Ye wild goats sporting round the eagle's nest!
Ye eagles, play-mates of the mountain-storm!
Ye lightnings, the dread arrows of the clouds!
Ye signs and wonders of the element!
Utter forth God, and fill the hills with praise!

Thou too, hoar Mount! with thy sky-pointing peak
Oft from whose feet the avalanche, unheard,
Shoots downward, glittering through the pure seren
Into the depth of clouds, that veil thy breast—
Thou too again, stupendous Mountain! thou
That as I raise my head, awhile bowed low
In adoration, upward from thy base
Slow travelling with dim eyes suffused with tears,
Solemnly seemest, like a vapoury cloud,
To rise before me—Rise, O ever rise,
Rise like a cloud of incense from the Earth!
Thou kingly Spirit throned among the hills,
Thou dread ambassador from Earth to Heaven,
Great hierarch! tell thou the silent sky,
And tell the stars, and tell yon rising sun
Earth, with her thousand voices, praises GOD.

III.

THE ANCIENT MARINER
AND OTHER POEMS.

THE RIME OF THE ANCIENT MARINER.

IN SEVEN PARTS.

ARGUMENT.

How a Ship having passed the Line was driven by storms to the cold Country towards the South Pole; and how from thence she made her course to the tropical Latitude of the Great Pacific Ocean; and of the strange things that befell; and in what manner the Ancyent Marinere came back to his own Country. [1798.]

PART I.

It is an ancient Mariner,
And he stoppeth one of three.
'By thy long grey beard and glittering eye,
Now wherefore stopp'st thou me?

The Bridegroom's doors are opened wide,
And I am next of kin;
The guests are met, the feast is set:
May'st hear the merry din.'

He holds him with his skinny hand,
'There was a ship,' quoth he.
'Hold off! unhand me, grey-beard loon!'
Eftsoons his hand dropt he.

He holds him with his glittering eye—
The Wedding-Guest stood still,
And listens like a three years' child:
The Mariner hath his will.

[margin note, handwritten:] Mariner = at wedding party, telling a tale

[margin gloss:] An ancient Mariner meeteth three Gallants bidden to a wedding-feast, and detaineth one.

[margin gloss:] The Wedding-Guest is spell-bound by the eye of the old sea-faring man, and constrained to hear his tale.

121

The Wedding-Guest sat on a stone:
He cannot choose but hear;
And thus spake on that ancient man,
The bright-eyed Mariner.

' The ship was cheered, the harbour cleared,
Merrily did we drop
Below the kirk, below the hill,
Below the lighthouse top.

The sun came up upon the left,
Out of the sea came he!
And he shone bright, and on the right
Went down into the sea.

The sun?

Higher and higher every day,
Till over the mast at noon—'
The Wedding-Guest here beat his breast,
For he heard the loud bassoon.

The bride had paced into the hall,
Red as a rose is she;
Nodding their heads before her goes
The merry minstrelsy.

The Wedding-Guest he beat his breast,
Yet he cannot choose but hear;
And thus spake on that ancient man,
The bright-eyed Mariner.

' And now the Storm-blast came, and he
Was tyrannous and strong:
He struck with his o'ertaking wings,
And chased us south along.

*Storm came +
pushed boat to S. pole*

The Mariner
tells how the
ship sailed
outward
with a good
wind and fair
weather, till
it reached
the line.

The Wed-
ding-Guest
heareth the
bridal music;
but the Mar-
iner con-
tinueth his
tale.

The ship
driven by a
storm toward
the south
pole.

With sloping masts and dipping prow,
As who pursued with yell and blow
Still treads the shadow of his foe,
And forward bends his head,
The ship drove fast, loud roared the blast,
And southward aye we fled.

And now there came both mist and snow,
And it grew wondrous cold:
And ice, mast-high, came floating by,
As green as emerald.

And through the drifts the snowy clifts
Did send a dismal sheen:
Nor shapes of men nor beasts we ken—
The ice was all between.

The land of ice, and of fearful sounds where no living thing was to be seen.

The ice was here, the ice was there,
The ice was all around:
It cracked and growled, and roared and howled,
Like noises in a swound!

At length did cross an Albatross, bird
Thorough the fog it came;
As if it had been a Christian soul,
We hailed it in God's name.

Till a great sea-bird, called the Albatross, came through the snow-fog, and was received with great joy and hospitality.

It ate the food it ne'er had eat,
And round and round it flew.
The ice did split with a thunder-fit;
The helmsman steered us through!

And a good south wind sprung up behind;
The Albatross did follow,
And every day, for food or play,
Came to the mariner's hollo!

And lo! the Albatross proveth a bird of good omen, and followeth the ship as it returned northward through fog and floating ice.

Albatross followed
their ship - good luck

In mist or cloud, on mast or shroud,
It perched for vespers nine;
Whiles all the night, through fog-smoke white,
Glimmered the white moon-shine.'

The ancient
Mariner in-
hospitably
killeth the
pious bird of
good omen.

' God save thee, ancient Mariner!
From the fiends, that plague thee thus!—
Why look'st thou so ? '—With my cross-bow
I shot the Albatross.

kills bird

PART II.

The Sun now rose upon the right:
Out of the sea came he,
Still hid in mist, and on the left
Went down into the sea.

And the good south wind still blew behind,
But no sweet bird did follow,
Nor any day for food or play
Came to the mariner's hollo!

His ship-
mates cry out
against the
ancient
Mariner, for
killing the
bird of good
luck.

And I had done a hellish thing,
And it would work 'em woe:
For all averred, I had killed the bird
That made the breeze to blow.
Ah wretch! said they, the bird to slay,
That made the breeze to blow!

But when the
fog cleared
off, they
justify the
same, and
thus make
themselves
accomplices
in the crime.

Nor dim nor red, like God's own head,
The glorious Sun uprist:
Then all averred, I had killed the bird
That brought the fog and mist.
'Twas right, said they, such birds to slay,
That bring the fog and mist.

The fair breeze blew, the white foam flew,
The furrow followed free;
We were the first that ever burst
Into that silent sea.

The fair
breeze con-
tinues; the
ship enters
the Pacific
Ocean, and
sails north-
ward, even
till it reaches
the Line.
The ship
hath been
suddenly be-
calmed.

Down dropt the breeze, the sails dropt down,
'Twas sad as sad could be;
And we did speak only to break
The silence of the sea!

sea becames calm

All in a hot and copper sky,
The bloody Sun, at noon,
Right up above the mast did stand,
No bigger than the Moon.

Day after day, day after day,
We stuck, nor breath nor motion;
As idle as a painted ship
Upon a painted ocean.

not. Moving

Water, water, every where,
And all the boards did shrink;
Water, water, every where
Nor any drop to drink.

wate

And the Al-
batross be-
gins to be
avenged.

The very deep did rot: O Christ!
That ever this should be!
Yea, slimy things did crawl with legs
Upon the slimy sea.

About, about, in reel and rout
The death-fires danced at night;
The water, like a witch's oils,
Burnt green, and blue and white.

And some in dreams assured were
Of the Spirit that plagued us so,
Nine fathom deep he had followed us
From the land of mist and snow.

And every tongue, through utter drought
Was withered at the root;
We could not speak, no more than if
We had been choked with soot.

Ah! well a-day! what evil looks
Had I from old and young!
Instead of the cross, the Albatross
About my neck was hung.

A Spirit had followed them; one of the invisible inhabitants of this planet, neither departed souls nor angels; concerning whom the learned Jew, Josephus, and the Platonic Constantinopolitan, Michael Psellus, may be consulted. They are very numerous, and there is no climate or element without one or more.

The ship-mates, in their sore distress, would fain throw the whole guilt on the ancient Mariner: in sign whereof they hang the dead sea-bird round his neck.

Part III.

There passed a weary time.   Each throat
Was parched, and glazed each eye.
A weary time! a weary time!
How glazed each weary eye,
When looking westward, I beheld
A something in the sky.

The Ancient Mariner beholdeth a sign in the element afar off.

At first it seemed a little speck,
And then it seemed a mist;
It moved and moved, and took at last
A certain shape, I wist.

A speck, a mist, a shape, I wist!
And still it neared and neared:
As if it dodged a water-sprite,
It plunged and tacked and veered.

With throats unslaked, with black lips baked,
We could nor laugh nor wail;
Through utter drought all dumb we stood!
I bit my arm, I sucked the blood,
And cried, A sail! a sail!

At its nearer approach, it seemeth him to be a ship; and at a dear ransom he freeth his speech from the bonds of thirst.

With throats unslaked, with black lips baked,
Agape they heard me call;
Gramercy! they for joy did grin,
And all at once their breath drew in,
As they were drinking all.

A flash of joy;

See! see! (I cried) she tacks no more!
Hither to work us weal;
Without a breeze, without a tide,
She steadies with upright keel!

] ship not moving

And horror follows. For can it be a ship that comes onward without wind or tide?

The western wave was all a-flame.
The day was well nigh done!
Almost upon the western wave
Rested the broad bright Sun;
When that strange shape drove suddenly
Betwixt us and the Sun.

And straight the Sun was flecked with bars,
(Heaven's Mother send us grace!)
As if through a dungeon-grate he peered
With broad and burning face.

It seemeth him but the skeleton of a ship.

Alas! (thought I, and my heart beat loud)
How fast she nears and nears!
Are those her sails that glance in the Sun,
Like restless gossameres?

And its ribs
are seen as
bars on the
face of the
setting Sun.

The Spectre-
Woman and
her Death-
mate, and no
other on
board the
skeleton-
ship.

Like vessel,
like crew!

Are those her ribs through which the Sun
Did peer, as through a grate?
And is that Woman all her crew?
Is that a Death? and are there two?
Is Death that woman's mate?

Her lips were red, her looks were free,
Her locks were yellow as gold:
Her skin was as white as leprosy,
The Night-mare Life-in-Death was she,
Who thicks man's blood with cold.

Scar
woma
=
Deatḥ

Death and
Life-in-
Death have
diced for the
ship's crew,
and she (the
latter)
winneth the
ancient
Mariner.

The naked hulk alongside came,
And the twain were casting dice;
'The game is done! I've won! I've won!'
Quoth she, and whistles thrice.

No twilight
within the
courts of the
Sun.

The Sun's rim dips; the stars rush out:
At one stride comes the dark;
With far-heard whisper, o'er the sea,
Off shot the spectre-bark.

At the rising
of the Moon,

We listened and looked sideways up!
Fear at my heart, as at a cup,
My life-blood seemed to sip!
The stars were dim, and thick the night,
The steersman's face by his lamp gleamed white;
From the sails the dew did drip—
Till clomb above the eastern bar
The horned Moon, with one bright star
Within the nether tip.

One after one, by the star-dogged Moon,
Too quick for groan or sigh,
Each turned his face with a ghastly pang,
And cursed me with his eye.

One after
another,

Four times fifty living men,
(And I heard nor sigh nor groan)
With heavy thump, a lifeless lump, *they*
They dropped down one by one. *die*

His ship-
mates drop
down dead.

The souls did from their bodies fly,—
They fled to bliss or woe!
And every soul, it passed me by,
Like the whizz of my cross-bow!

*the souls
flying out of
bodies*

But Life-in-
Death
begins her
work on the
ancient
Mariner,

Part IV.

' I fear thee, ancient Mariner!
I fear thy skinny hand!
And thou art long, and lank, and brown,
As is the ribbed sea-sand.

The Wed-
ding-Guest
feareth that
a Spirit is
talking to
him;

I fear thee and thy glittering eye,
And thy skinny hand, so brown.'—
Fear not, fear not, thou Wedding-Guest!
This body dropt not down.

But the
ancient
Mariner as-
sureth him
of his bodily
life, and pro-
ceedeth to
relate his
horrible pen-
ance.

Alone, alone, all, all alone,
Alone on a wide wide sea!
And never a saint took pity on
My soul in agony.

*revenge from the bird on Mariner-
at sea all alone*

He despiseth
the creatures
of the calm.

The many men, so beautiful!
And they all dead did lie:
And a thousand thousand slimy things
Lived on; and so did I.

And envieth
that they
should live,
and so many
lie dead.

I looked upon the rotting sea,
And drew my eyes away;
I looked upon the rotting deck,
And there the dead men lay.

I looked to heaven, and tried to pray;
But or ever a prayer had gusht,
A wicked whisper came, and made
My heart as dry as dust.

I closed my lids, and kept them close,
And the balls like pulses beat;
For the sky and the sea, and the sea and the s]
Lay like a load on my weary eye,
And the dead were at my feet.

But the
curse liveth
for him in
the eye of
the dead
men.

The cold sweat melted from their limbs,
Nor rot nor rook did they:
The look with which they looked on me
Had never passed away.

An orphan's curse would drag to hell
A spirit from on high;
But oh! more horrible than that
Is the curse in a dead man's eye!
Seven days, seven nights, I saw that curse,
And yet I could not die.

The moving Moon went up the sky,
And no where did abide:
Softly she was going up,
And a star or two beside—

Her beams bemocked the sultry main,
Like April hoar-frost spread;
But where the ship's huge shadow lay,
The charmed water burnt alway
A still and awful red.

Beyond the shadow of the ship,
I watched the water-snakes:
They moved in tracks of shining white,
And when they reared, the elfish light
Fell off in hoary flakes.

Within the shadow of the ship
I watched their rich attire:
Blue, glossy green, and velvet black,
They coiled and swam; and every track
Was a flash of golden fire.

O happy living things! no tongue
Their beauty might declare:
A spring of love gushed from my heart,
And I blessed them unaware:
Sure my kind saint took pity on me,
And I blessed them unaware.

The selfsame moment I could pray;
And from my neck so free
The Albatross fell off, and sank
Like lead into the sea.

In his loneliness and fixedness he yearneth towards the journeying Moon, and the stars that still sojourn, yet still move onward; and everywhere the blue sky belongs to them, and is their appointed rest, and their native country and their own natural homes, which they enter unannounced, as lords that are certainly expected and yet there is a silent joy at their arrival.

By the light of the Moon he beholdeth God's creatures of the great calm.

Their beauty and their happiness.

He blesseth them in his heart.

The spell begins to break.

He is making peace w/ the animals

→ curse wears off

I 43

PART V.

Oh sleep! it is a gentle thing,
Beloved from pole to pole!
To Mary Queen the praise be given!
She sent the gentle sleep from Heaven,
That slid into my soul.

By grace of the holy Mother, the ancient Mariner is refreshed with rain.

The silly buckets on the deck,
That had so long remained,
I dreamt that they were filled with dew;
And when I awoke, it rained.

is he dying?

My lips were wet, my throat was cold,
My garments all were dank;
Sure I had drunken in my dreams,
And still my body drank.

I moved, and could not feel my limbs;
I was so light—almost
I thought that I had died in sleep,
And was a blessed ghost.

He heareth sounds and seeth strange sights and commotions in the sky and the element.

And soon I heard a roaring wind:
It did not come anear;
But with its sound it shook the sails,
That were so thin and sere.

The upper air burst into life!
And a hundred fire-flags sheen,
To and fro they were hurried about!
And to and fro, and in and out,
The wan stars danced between.

And the coming wind did roar more loud,
And the sails did sigh like sedge;
And the rain poured down from one black cloud;
The Moon was at its edge.

The thick black cloud was cleft, and still
The Moon was at its side:
Like waters shot from some high crag,
The lightning fell with never a jag,
A river steep and wide.

The loud wind never reached the ship,
Yet now the ship moved on!
Beneath the lightning and the Moon
The dead men gave a groan.

The bodies of the ship's crew are inspired, and the ship moves on;

They groaned, they stirred, they all uprose,
Nor spake, nor moved their eyes;
It had been strange, even in a dream,
To have seen those dead men rise.

The helmsman steered, the ship moved on;
Yet never a breeze up blew;
The mariners all 'gan work the ropes,
Where they were wont to do;
They raised their limbs like lifeless tools—
We were a ghastly crew.

The body of my brother's son
Stood by me, knee to knee:
The body and I pulled at one rope
But he said nought to me.

But not by
the souls of
the men, nor
by dæmons
of earth or
middle air,
but by a
blessed troop
of angelic
spirits, sent
down by the
invocation of
the guardian
saint.

' I fear thee, ancient Mariner ! '
Be calm, thou Wedding-Guest !
'Twas not those souls that fled in pain,
Which to their corses came again,
But a troop of spirits blest :

For when it dawned—they dropped their arms,
And clustered round the mast ;
Sweet sounds rose slowly through their mouths,
And from their bodies passed.

Around, around, flew each sweet sound,
Then darted to the Sun ;
Slowly the sounds came back again,
Now mixed, now one by one.

Sometimes a-dropping from the sky
I heard the sky-lark sing ;
Sometimes all little birds that are,
How they seemed to fill the sea and air
With their sweet jargoning !

And now 'twas like all instruments,
Now like a lonely flute ;
And now it is an angel's song,
That makes the heavens be mute.

It ceased ; yet still the sails made on
A pleasant noise till noon,
A noise like of a hidden brook
In the leafy month of June,
That to the sleeping woods all night
Singeth a quiet tune.

Till noon we quietly sailed on,
Yet never a breeze did breathe:
Slowly and smoothly went the ship,
Moved onward from beneath.

Under the keel nine fathom deep,
From the land of mist and snow,
The spirit slid: and it was he
That made the ship to go.
The sails at noon left off their tune,
And the ship stood still also.

The lonesome Spirit from the south-pole carries on the ship as far as the Line, in obedience to the angelic troop, but still requireth vengeance.

The Sun, right up above the mast,
Had fixed her to the ocean:
But in a minute she 'gan stir,
With a short uneasy motion—
Backwards and forwards half her length
With a short uneasy motion.

Then like a pawing horse let go,
She made a sudden bound:
It flung the blood into my head,
And I fell down in a swound.

How long in that same fit I lay,
I have not to declare;
But ere my living life returned,
I heard and in my soul discerned
Two voices in the air.

The Polar Spirit's fellow-dæmons, the invisible inhabitants of the element, take part in his wrong; and two of them relate, one to the other, that penance long and heavy for the ancient Mariner hath been accorded to the Polar Spirit, who returneth southward.

' Is it he ? ' quoth one, ' Is this the man ?
By him who died on cross,
With his cruel bow he laid full low
The harmless Albatross.

spirits talking about him

The spirit who bideth by himself
In the land of mist and snow,
He loved the bird that loved the man
Who shot him with his bow.'

The other was a softer voice,
As soft as honey-dew:
Quoth he, 'The man hath penance done,
And penance more will do.'

PART VI.

FIRST VOICE.

' But tell me, tell me! speak again,
Thy soft response renewing—
What makes that ship drive on so fast?
What is the ocean doing?'

SECOND VOICE.

' Still as a slave before his lord,
The ocean hath no blast;
His great bright eye most silently
Up to the moon is cast—

If he may know which way to go;
For she guides him smooth or grim.
See, brother, see! how graciously
She looketh down on him.'

FIRST VOICE.

' But why drives on that ship so fast,
Without or wave or wind?'

The Mariner
hath been
cast into a
trance; for
the angelic
power caus-
eth the vessel
to drive
northward
faster than
human life
could en-
dure.

SECOND VOICE.

' The air is cut away before,
And closes from behind.

Fly, brother, fly! more high, more high!
Or we shall be belated:
For slow and slow that ship will go,
When the Mariner's trance is abated.'

I woke, and we were sailing on
As in a gentle weather:
'Twas night, calm night, the moon was high,
The dead men stood together.

The super-
natural
motion is
retarded;
the Mariner
awakes, and
his penance
begins anew.

All stood together on the deck,
For a charnel-dungeon fitter:
All fixed on me their stony eyes,
That in the Moon did glitter.

The pang, the curse, with which they died,
Had never passed away:
I could not draw my eyes from theirs,
Nor turn them up to pray.

And now this spell was snapt: once more
I viewed the ocean green,
And looked far forth, yet little saw
Of what had else been seen—

The curse is
finally ex-
piated.

Like one, that on a lonesome road
Doth walk in fear and dread,
And having once turned round walks on,
And turns no more his head;
Because he knows, a frightful fiend
Doth close behind him tread.

But soon there breathed a wind on me,
Nor sound nor motion made:
Its path was not upon the sea,
In ripple or in shade.

It raised my hair, it fanned my cheek
Like a meadow-gale of spring—
It mingled strangely with my fears,
Yet it felt like a welcoming.

Swiftly, swiftly flew the ship,
Yet she sailed softly too:
Sweetly, sweetly blew the breeze—
On me alone it blew.

And the
ancient Ma-
riner be-
holdeth his
native
country.

Oh! dream of joy! is this indeed
The light-house top I see?
Is this the hill? is this the kirk?
Is this mine own countree?

We drifted o'er the harbour-bar,
And I with sobs did pray—
O let me be awake, my God!
Or let me sleep alway.

The harbour-bay was clear as glass,
So smoothly it was strewn!
And on the bay the moonlight lay,
And the shadow of the Moon.

The rock shone bright, the kirk no less,
That stands above the rock:
The <u>moonlight</u> steeped in silentness
The steady weathercock.

And the bay was white with silent light
Till rising from the same,
Full many shapes, that shadows were,
In crimson colours came.

The Angelic
spirits leave
the dead
bodies,

A little distance from the prow
Those crimson shadows were:
I turned my eyes upon the deck—
Oh, Christ! what saw I there!

And appear
in their own
forms of light

spirits
reappear
as light.

Each corse lay flat, lifeless and flat,
And, by the holy rood!
A man all light, a seraph-man,
On every corse there stood.

This seraph-band, each waved his hand;
It was a heavenly sight!
They stood as signals to the land,
Each one a lovely light;

This seraph-band, each waved his hand,
No voice did they impart—
No voice; but oh! the silence sank
Like music on my heart.

But soon I heard the dash of oars,
I heard the Pilot's cheer;
My head was turned perforce away,
And I saw a boat appear.

The Pilot and the Pilot's boy,
I heard them coming fast:
Dear Lord in Heaven! it was a joy
The dead men could not blast.

I saw a third—I heard his voice:
It is the Hermit good!
He singeth loud his godly hymns
That he makes in the wood.
He'll shrieve my soul, he'll wash away
The Albatross's blood.

PART VII.

The Hermit
of the Wood.

This Hermit good lives in that wood
Which slopes down to the sea.
How loudly his sweet voice he rears!
He loves to talk with marineres
That come from a far countree.

He kneels at morn, and noon, and eve—
He hath a cushion plump:
It is the moss that wholly hides
The rotted old oak-stump.

The skiff-boat neared: I heard them talk,
'Why, this is strange, I trow!
Where are those lights so many and fair,
That signal made but now?'

' Strange, by my faith!' the Hermit said—
' And they answered not our cheer!
The planks look warped! and see those sails,
How thin they are and sere!
I never saw aught like to them,
Unless perchance it were

Brown skeletons of leaves that lag
My forest-brook along;
When the ivy-tod is heavy with snow,
And the owlet whoops to the wolf below,
That eats the she-wolf's young.'

' Dear Lord! it hath a fiendish look—
(The Pilot made reply)
I am a-feared '—' Push on, push on!'
Said the Hermit cheerily.

The boat came closer to the ship,
But I nor spake nor stirred;
The boat came close beneath the ship,
And straight a sound was heard.

Under the water it rumbled on,
Still louder and more dread:
It reached the ship, it split the bay;
The ship went down like lead.

Stunned by that loud and dreadful sound,
Which sky and ocean smote,
Like one that hath been seven days drowned
My body lay afloat;
But swift as dreams, myself I found
Within the Pilot's boat.

Marginal glosses:

Approacheth the ship with wonder.

The ship suddenly sinketh.

The ancient Mariner is saved in the Pilot's boat.

Upon the whirl, where sank the ship,
The boat spun round and round;
And all was still, save that the hill
Was telling of the sound.

I moved my lips—the Pilot shrieked
And fell down in a fit;
The holy Hermit raised his eyes,
And prayed where he did sit.

I took the oars: the Pilot's boy,
Who now doth crazy go,
Laughed loud and long, and all the while
His eyes went to and fro.
'Ha! ha!' quoth he, 'full plain I see,
The Devil knows how to row.'

And now, all in my own countree,
I stood on the firm land!
The Hermit stepped forth from the boat,
And scarcely he could stand.

The ancient
Mariner
earnestly en-
treateth the
Hermit to
shrieve him;
and the
penance of
life falls on
him.

'O shrieve me, shrieve me, holy man!'
The Hermit crossed his brow.
'Say quick,' quoth he, 'I bid thee say—
What manner of man art thou?'

Forthwith this frame of mine was wrenched
With a woful agony,
Which forced me to begin my tale;
And then it left me free.

Since then, at an uncertain hour,
That agony returns:
And till my ghastly tale is told,
This heart within me burns.

And ever
and anon
throughout
his future life
an agony
constraineth
him to travel
from land to
land,

I pass, like night, from land to land;
I have strange power of speech;
That moment that his face I see,
I know the man that must hear me:
To him my tale I teach.

What loud uproar bursts from that door!
The wedding-guests are there:
But in the garden-bower the bride
And bride-maids singing are:
And hark the little vesper bell
Which biddeth me to prayer!

O Wedding-Guest! this soul hath been
Alone on a wide wide sea;
So lonely 'twas, that God himself
Scarce seemed there to be.

O sweeter than the marriage-feast,
'Tis sweeter far to me,
To walk together to the kirk
With a goodly company!—

To walk together to the kirk,
And all together pray,
While each to his great Father bends,
Old men, and babes, and loving friends,
And youths and maidens gay!

And to teach,
by his own
example,
love and re-
verence to all
things that
God made
and loveth.

Farewell, farewell! but this I tell
To thee, thou Wedding-Guest!
He prayeth well, who loveth well
Both man and bird and beast.

He prayeth best, who loveth best
All things both great and small;
For the dear God who loveth us,
He made and loveth all.

The Mariner, whose eye is bright,
Whose beard with age is hoar,
Is gone: and now the Wedding-Guest
Turned from the bridegroom's door.

He went like one that hath been stunned,
And is of sense forlorn:
A sadder and a wiser man,
He rose the morrow morn.

1797-1798.

THE RAVEN.

A CHRISTMAS TALE, TOLD BY A SCHOOL-BOY TO
HIS LITTLE BROTHERS AND SISTERS.

UNDERNEATH a huge oak tree
There was of swine a huge company,
That grunted as they crunched the mast:
For that was ripe, and fell full fast.
Then they trotted away, for the wind grew high:
One acorn they left, and no more might you spy.
Next came a Raven, that liked not such folly:
He belonged, they did say, to the witch Melancholy!
Blacker was he than blackest jet,
Flew low in the rain, and his feathers not wet.
He picked up the acorn and buried it straight
By the side of a river both deep and great.
      Where then did the Raven go?
      He went high and low,
   Over hill, over dale, did the black Raven go.
     Many Autumns, many Springs
     Travelled he with wandering wings:
     Many Summers, many Winters—
     I can't tell half his adventures.

At length he came back, and with him a She,
And the acorn was grown to a tall oak tree.
They built them a nest in the topmost bough,
And young ones they had, and were happy enow.

But soon came a woodman in leathern guise,
His brow, like a pent-house, hung over his eyes.
He'd an axe in his hand, not a word he spoke,
But with many a hem! and a sturdy stroke,
At length he brought down the poor Raven's own oa
His young ones were killed; for they could not depar
And their mother did die of a broken heart.

The boughs from the trunk the woodman did sever
And they floated it down on the course of the river
They sawed it in planks, and its bark they did strip
And with this tree and others they made a good ship
The ship, it was launched; but in sight of the lan
Such a storm there did rise as no ship could withsta
It bulged on a rock, and the waves rush'd in fast
The old Raven flew round and round, and cawed
       the blast.

He heard the last shriek of the perishing souls—
See! see! o'er the topmast the mad water rolls!
   Right glad was the Raven, and off he went fleet
And Death riding home on a cloud he did meet,
   And he thank'd him again and again for this treat
      They had taken his all, and REVENGE WAS SWEET

                                          ? 179

CHRISTABEL.

PART THE FIRST.

'Tis the middle of night by the castle clock,
And the owls have awakened the crowing cock,
Tu—whit!——Tu—whoo!
And hark, again! the crowing cock,
How drowsily it crew.

Sir Leoline, the Baron rich,
Hath a toothless mastiff, which
From her kennel beneath the rock
Maketh answer to the clock,
Four for the quarters, and twelve for the hour;
Ever and aye, by shine and shower,
Sixteen short howls, not over loud;
Some say, she sees my lady's shroud.

Is the night chilly and dark?
The night is chilly, but not dark.
The thin gray cloud is spread on high,
It covers but not hides the sky.
The moon is behind, and at the full;
And yet she looks both small and dull.
The night is chill, the cloud is gray:
'Tis a month before the month of May,
And the Spring comes slowly up this way.

The lovely lady, Christabel,
Whom her father loves so well,
What makes her in the wood so late,
A furlong from the castle gate?
She had dreams all yesternight
Of her own betrothed knight;
And she in the midnight wood will pray
For the weal of her lover that's far away.

She stole along, she nothing spoke,
The sighs she heaved were soft and low,
And nought was green upon the oak
But moss and rarest mistletoe:
She kneels beneath the huge oak tree,
And in silence prayeth she.

The lady sprang up suddenly,
The lovely lady, Christabel!
It moaned as near, as near can be,
But what it is she cannot tell.—
On the other side it seems to be,
Of the huge, broad-breasted, old oak tree.

The night is chill; the forest bare;
Is it the wind that moaneth bleak?
There is not wind enough in the air
To move away the ringlet curl
From the lovely lady's cheek—

There is not wind enough to twirl
The one red leaf, the last of its clan,
That dances as often as dance it can,
Hanging so light, and hanging so high,
On the topmast twig that looks up at the sky.

Hush, beating heart of Christabel!
Jesu, Maria, shield her well!
She folded her arms beneath her cloak,
And stole to the other side of the oak.
     What sees she there?

There she sees a damsel bright,
Drest in a silken robe of white,
That shadowy in the moonlight shone:
The neck that made that white robe wan,
Her stately neck, and arms were bare;
Her blue-veined feet unsandal'd were,
And wildly glittered here and there
The gems entangled in her hair.
I guess, 'twas frightful there to see
A lady so richly clad as she—
Beautiful exceedingly!

Mary mother, save me now!
(Said Christabel,) And who art thou?

The lady strange made answer meet,
And her voice was faint and sweet:—
Have pity on my sore distress,
I scarce can speak for weariness:
Stretch forth thy hand, and have no fear!
Said Christabel, How camest thou here?
And the lady, whose voice was faint and sweet,
Did thus pursue her answer meet:—

My sire is of a noble line,
And my name is Geraldine:—
Five warriors seized me yestermorn,
Me, even me, a maid forlorn:

They choked my cries with force and fright,
And tied me on a palfrey white.
The palfrey was as fleet as wind,
And they rode furiously behind.
They spurred amain, their steeds were white:
And once we crossed the shade of night.
As sure as Heaven shall rescue me,
I have no thought what men they be;
Nor do I know how long it is
(For I have lain entranced I wis)
Since one, the tallest of the five,
Took me from the palfrey's back,
A weary woman, scarce alive.
Some muttered words his comrades spoke:
He placed me underneath this oak;
He swore they would return with haste;
Whither they went I cannot tell—
I thought I heard, some minutes past,
Sounds as of a castle bell.
Stretch forth thy hand (thus ended she),
And help a wretched maid to flee.

Then Christabel stretched forth her hand,
And comforted fair Geraldine:
O well, bright dame! may you command
The service of Sir Leoline;
And gladly our stout chivalry
Will he send forth and friends withal
To guide and guard you safe and free
Home to your noble father's hall.

She rose: and forth with steps they passed
That strove to be, and were not, fast.

Her gracious stars the lady blest,
And thus spake on sweet Christabel:
All our household are at rest,
The hall as silent as the cell;
Sir Leoline is weak in health,
And may not well awakened be,
But we will move as if in stealth,
And I beseech your courtesy,
This night, to share your couch with me.

They crossed the moat, and Christabel
Took the key that fitted well;
A little door she opened straight,
All in the middle of the gate;
The gate that was ironed within and without,
Where an army in battle array had marched out.
The lady sank, belike through pain,
And Christabel with might and main
Lifted her up, a weary weight,
Over the threshold of the gate:
Then the lady rose again,
And moved, as she were not in pain.

So free from danger, free from fear,
They crossed the court: right glad they were.
And Christabel devoutly cried
To the lady by her side,
Praise we the Virgin all divine
Who hath rescued thee from thy distress!
Alas, alas! said Geraldine,
I cannot speak for weariness.
So free from danger, free from fear,
They crossed the court: right glad they were.

Outside her kennel, the mastiff old
Lay fast asleep, in moonshine cold.
The mastiff old did not awake,
Yet she an angry moan did make!
And what can ail the mastiff bitch?
Never till now she uttered yell
Beneath the eye of Christabel.
Perhaps it is the owlet's scritch:
For what can ail the mastiff bitch?

They passed the hall, that echoes still,
Pass as lightly as you will!
The brands were flat, the brands were dying,
Amid their own white ashes lying;
But when the lady passed, there came
A tongue of light, a fit of flame;
And Christabel saw the lady's eye,
And nothing else saw she thereby,
Save the boss of the shield of Sir Leoline tall,
Which hung in a murky old niche in the wall.
O softly tread, said Christabel,
My father seldom sleepeth well.

Sweet Christabel her feet doth bare,
And jealous of the listening air
They steal their way from stair to stair,
Now in glimmer, and now in gloom,
And now they pass the Baron's room,
As still as death, with stifled breath!
And now have reached her chamber door;
And now doth Geraldine press down
The rushes of the chamber floor.

The moon shines dim in the open air,
And not a moonbeam enters here.
But they without its light can see
The chamber carved so curiously,
Carved with figures strange and sweet,
All made out of the carver's brain,
For a lady's chamber meet:
The lamp with twofold silver chain
Is fastened to an angel's feet.

The silver lamp burns dead and dim;
But Christabel the lamp will trim.
She trimmed the lamp, and made it bright,
And left it swinging to and fro,
While Geraldine, in wretched plight,
Sank down upon the floor below.

O weary lady, Geraldine,
I pray you, drink this cordial wine!
It is a wine of virtuous powers;
My mother made it of wild flowers.

And will your mother pity me,
Who am a maiden most forlorn?
Christabel answered—Woe is me!
She died the hour that I was born.
I have heard the grey-haired friar tell
How on her death-bed she did say,
That she should hear the castle-bell
Strike twelve upon my wedding-day.
O mother dear! that thou wert here!
I would, said Geraldine, she were!

But soon with altered voice, said she—
' Off, wandering mother!   Peak and pine!
I have power to bid thee flee.'
Alas! what ails poor Geraldine?
Why stares she with unsettled eye?
Can she the bodiless dead espy?
And why with hollow voice cries she,
' Off, woman, off! this hour is mine—
Though thou her guardian spirit be,
Off, woman, off! 'tis given to me.'

Then Christabel knelt by the lady's side,
And raised to heaven her eyes so blue—
Alas! said she, this ghastly ride—
Dear lady! it hath wildered you!
The lady wiped her moist cold brow,
And faintly said, ' 'tis over now! '

Again the wild-flower wine she drank:
Her fair large eyes 'gan glitter bright,
And from the floor whereon she sank,
The lofty lady stood upright:
She was most beautiful to see,
Like a lady of a far countree.

And thus the lofty lady spake—
' All they who live in the upper sky,
Do love you, holy Christabel!
And you love them, and for their sake
And for the good which me befel,
Even I in my degree will try,
Fair maiden, to requite you well.
But now unrobe yourself; for I
Must pray, ere yet in bed I lie.'

Quoth Christabel, So let it be!
And as the lady bade, did she.
Her gentle limbs did she undress,
And lay down in her loveliness.

But through her brain of weal and woe
So many thoughts moved to and fro,
That vain it were her lids to close;
So half-way from the bed she rose,
And on her elbow did recline
To look at the lady Geraldine.

Beneath the lamp the lady bowed,
And slowly rolled her eyes around;
Then drawing in her breath aloud,
Like one that shuddered, she unbound
The cincture from beneath her breast:
Her silken robe, and inner vest,
Dropt to her feet, and full in view,
Behold! her bosom and half her side——
A sight to dream of, not to tell!
O shield her! shield sweet Christabel!

Yet Geraldine nor speaks nor stirs;
Ah! what a stricken look was hers!
Deep from within she seems half-way
To lift some weight with sick assay,
And eyes the maid and seeks delay;
Then suddenly, as one defied,
Collects herself in scorn and pride,
And lay down by the Maiden's side!—
And in her arms the maid she took,
　　　　Ah well-a-day!
And with low voice and doleful look
These words did say:

'In the touch of this bosom there worketh a spell,
Which is lord of thy utterance, Christabel!
Thou knowest to-night, and wilt know to-morrow,
This mark of my shame, this seal of my sorrow;
     But vainly thou warrest,
      For this is alone in
     Thy power to declare,
      That in the dim forest
     Thou heard'st a low moaning,
And found'st a bright lady, surpassingly fair;
And didst bring her home with thee in love and
   in charity,
To shield her and shelter her from the damp air.'

THE CONCLUSION TO PART THE FIRST.

It was a lovely sight to see
The lady Christabel, when she
Was praying at the old oak tree.
     Amid the jagged shadows
     Of mossy leafless boughs,
     Kneeling in the moonlight,
     To make her gentle vows;
Her slender palms together prest,
Heaving sometimes on her breast;
Her face resigned to bliss or bale—
Her face, oh call it fair not pale,
And both blue eyes more bright than clear,
Each about to have a tear.

With open eyes (ah woe is me!)
Asleep, and dreaming fearfully,
Fearfully dreaming, yet, I wis,
Dreaming that alone, which is—

O sorrow and shame! Can this be she,
The lady, who knelt at the old oak tree?
And lo! the worker of these harms,
That holds the maiden in her arms,
Seems to slumber still and mild,
As a mother with her child.

A star hath set, a star hath risen,
O Geraldine! since arms of thine
Have been the lovely lady's prison.
O Geraldine! one hour was thine—
Thou'st had thy will! By tairn and rill,
The night-birds all that hour were still.
But now they are jubilant anew,
From cliff and tower, tu—whoo! tu—whoo!
Tu—whoo! tu—whoo! from wood and fell!

And see! the lady Christabel
Gathers herself from out her trance;
Her limbs relax, her countenance
Grows sad and soft; the smooth thin lids
Close o'er her eyes; and tears she sheds—
Large tears that leave the lashes bright!
And oft the while she seems to smile
As infants at a sudden light!

Yea, she doth smile, and she doth weep,
Like a youthful hermitess,
Beauteous in a wilderness,
Who, praying always, prays in sleep.
And, if she move unquietly,
Perchance, 'tis but the blood so free
Comes back and tingles in her feet.
No doubt, she hath a vision sweet.

What if her guardian spirit 'twere,
What if she knew her mother near?
But this she knows, in joys and woes,
That saints will aid if men will call:
For the blue sky bends over all!

1797.

PART THE SECOND.

Each matin bell, the Baron saith,
Knells us back to a world of death.
These words Sir Leoline first said,
When he rose and found his lady dead:
These words Sir Leoline will say
Many a morn to his dying day!

And hence the custom and law began
That still at dawn the sacristan,
Who duly pulls the heavy bell,
Five and forty beads must tell
Between each stroke—a warning knell,
Which not a soul can choose but hear
From Bratha Head to Wyndermere.

Saith Bracy the bard, So let it knell!
And let the drowsy sacristan
Still count as slowly as he can!
There is no lack of such, I ween,
As well fill up the space between.
In Langdale Pike and Witch's Lair,
And Dungeon-ghyll so foully rent,
With ropes of rock and bells of air
Three sinful sextons' ghosts are pent,

Who all give back, one after t'other,
The death-note to their living brother;
And oft too, by the knell offended,
Just as their one! two! three! is ended,
The devil mocks the doleful tale
With a merry peal from Borrowdale.

The air is still! through mist and cloud
That merry peal comes ringing loud;
And Geraldine shakes off her dread,
And rises lightly from the bed;
Puts on her silken vestments white,
And tricks her hair in lovely plight,
And nothing doubting of her spell
Awakens the lady Christabel.
' Sleep you, sweet lady Christabel?
I trust that you have rested well.'

And Christabel awoke and spied
The same who lay down by her side—
O rather say, the same whom she
Raised up beneath the old oak tree!
Nay, fairer yet! and yet more fair!
For she belike hath drunken deep
Of all the blessedness of sleep!
And while she spake, her looks, her air,
Such gentle thankfulness declare,
That (so it seemed) her girded vests
Grew tight beneath her heaving breasts.
' Sure I have sinn'd! " said Christabel,
' Now heaven be praised if all be well!'
And in low faltering tones, yet sweet,
Did she the lofty lady greet
With such perplexity of mind
As dreams too lively leave behind.

So quickly she rose, and quickly arrayed
Her maiden limbs, and having prayed
That He, who on the cross did groan,
Might wash away her sins unknown,
She forthwith led fair Geraldine
To meet her sire, Sir Leoline.

The lovely maid and the lady tall
Are pacing both into the hall,
And pacing on through page and groom,
Enter the Baron's presence-room.

The Baron rose, and while he prest
His gentle daughter to his breast,
With cheerful wonder in his eyes
The lady Geraldine espies,
And gave such welcome to the same,
As might beseem so bright a dame!

But when he heard the lady's tale,
And when she told her father's name,
Why waxed Sir Leoline so pale,
Murmuring o'er the name again,
Lord Roland de Vaux of Tryermaine?

Alas! they had been friends in youth;
But whispering tongues can poison truth;
And constancy lives in realms above;
And life is thorny; and youth is vain;
And to be wroth with one we love
Doth work like madness in the brain.
And thus it chanced, as I divine,
With Roland and Sir Leoline.

Each spake words of high disdain
And insult to his heart's best brother:
They parted—ne'er to meet again!
But never either found another
To free the hollow heart from paining—
They stood aloof, the scars remaining,
Like cliffs which had been rent asunder;
A dreary sea now flows between.
But neither heat, nor frost, nor thunder,
Shall wholly do away, I ween,
The marks of that which once hath been.

Sir Leoline, a moment's space,
Stood gazing on the damsel's face:
And the youthful Lord of Tryermaine
Came back upon his heart again.

O then the Baron forgot his age,
His noble heart swelled high with rage;
He swore by the wounds in Jesu's side
He would proclaim it far and wide,
With trump and solemn heraldry,
That they, who thus had wronged the dame
Were base as spotted infamy!
' And if they dare deny the same,
My herald shall appoint a week,
And let the recreant traitors seek
My tourney court—that there and then
I may dislodge their reptile souls
From the bodies and forms of men!'
He spake: his eye in lightning rolls!
For the lady was ruthlessly seized; and he kenned
In the beautiful lady the child of his friend!

And now the tears were on his face,
And fondly in his arms he took
Fair Geraldine, who met the embrace,
Prolonging it with joyous look.
Which when she viewed, a vision fell
Upon the soul of Christabel,
The vision of fear, the touch and pain!
She shrunk and shuddered, and saw again—
(Ah, woe is me! Was it for thee,
Thou gentle maid! such sights to see?)

Again she saw that bosom old,
Again she felt that bosom cold,
And drew in her breath with a hissing sound:
Whereat the Knight turned wildly round,
And nothing saw, but his own sweet maid
With eyes upraised, as one that prayed.

The touch, the sight, had passed away,
And in its stead that vision blest,
Which comforted her after-rest,
While in the lady's arms she lay,
Had put a rapture in her breast,
And on her lips and o'er her eyes
Spread smiles like light!
                              With new surprise,
' What ails then my beloved child? '
The Baron said—His daughter mild
Made answer, ' All will yet be well! '
I ween, she had no power to tell
Aught else: so mighty was the spell.
Yet he, who saw this Geraldine,
Had deemed her sure a thing divine.
Such sorrow with such grace she blended,
As if she feared she had offended

Sweet Christabel, that gentle maid!
And with such lowly tones she prayed
She might be sent without delay
Home to her father's mansion.

        ' Nay!
Nay, by my soul!' said Leoline.
' Ho! Bracy the bard, the charge be thine!
Go thou, with music sweet and loud,
And take two steeds with trappings proud,
And take the youth whom thou lov'st best
To bear thy harp, and learn thy song,
And clothe you both in solemn vest,
And over the mountains haste along,
Lest wandering folk, that are abroad,
Detain you on the valley road.

' And when he has crossed the Irthing flood,
My merry bard! he hastes, he hastes
Up Knorren Moor, through Halegarth Wood,
And reaches soon that castle good
Which stands and threatens Scotland's wastes.

' Bard Bracy! bard Bracy! your horses are fleet,
Ye must ride up the hall, your music so sweet,
More loud than your horses' echoing feet!
And loud and loud to Lord Roland call,
Thy daughter is safe in Langdale hall!
Thy beautiful daughter is safe and free—
Sir Leoline greets thee thus through me.
He bids thee come without delay
With all thy numerous array;
And take thy lovely daughter home:
And he will meet thee on the way
With all his numerous array
White with their panting palfreys' foam:

L 43

And, by mine honour! I will say,
That I repent me of the day
When I spake words of fierce disdain
To Roland de Vaux of Tryermaine!—
—For since that evil hour hath flown,
Many a summer's sun hath shone;
Yet ne'er found I a friend again
Like Roland de Vaux of Tryermaine.'

The lady fell, and clasped his knees,
Her face upraised, her eyes o'erflowing;
And Bracy replied, with faltering voice,
His gracious hail on all bestowing;
'Thy words, thou sire of Christabel,
Are sweeter than my harp can tell;
Yet might I gain a boon of thee,
This day my journey should not be,
So strange a dream hath come to me;
That I had vowed with music loud
To clear yon wood from thing unblest,
Warn'd by a vision in my rest!
For in my sleep I saw that dove,
That gentle bird, whom thou dost love,
And call'st by thy own daughter's name—
Sir Leoline! I saw the same,
Fluttering, and uttering fearful moan,
Among the green herbs in the forest alone.
Which when I saw and when I heard,
I wonder'd what might ail the bird;
For nothing near it could I see,
Save the grass and green herbs underneath
        the old tree.

'And in my dream, methought, I went
To search out what might there be found;
And what the sweet bird's trouble meant,
That thus lay fluttering on the ground.
I went and peered, and could descry
No cause for her distressful cry;
But yet for her dear lady's sake
I stooped, methought, the dove to take,
When lo! I saw a bright green snake
Coiled around its wings and neck,
Green as the herbs on which it couched,
Close by the dove's its head it crouched;
And with the dove it heaves and stirs,
Swelling its neck as she swelled hers!
I woke; it was the midnight hour,
The clock was echoing in the tower;
But though my slumber was gone by,
This dream it would not pass away—
It seems to live upon my eye!
And thence I vowed this self-same day
With music strong and saintly song
To wander through the forest bare,
Lest aught unholy loiter there.'

Thus Bracy said: the Baron, the while,
Half-listening heard him with a smile;
Then turned to Lady Geraldine,
His eyes made up of wonder and love;
And said in courtly accents fine,
'Sweet maid, Lord Roland's beauteous dove,
With arms more strong than harp or song,
Thy sire and I will crush the snake!'
He kissed her forehead as he spake,

And Geraldine in maiden wise
Casting down her large bright eyes,
With blushing cheek and courtesy fine
She turned her from Sir Leoline;
Softly gathering up her train,
That o'er her right arm fell again;
And folded her arms across her chest,
And couched her head upon her breast,
And looked askance at Christabel——
Jesu, Maria, shield her well!

A snake's small eye blinks dull and shy,
And the lady's eyes they shrunk in her head,
Each shrunk up to a serpent's eye,
And with somewhat of malice, and more of dread,
At Christabel she look'd askance!—
One moment—and the sight was fled!
But Christabel in dizzy trance
Stumbling on the unsteady ground
Shuddered aloud, with a hissing sound;
And Geraldine again turned round,
And like a thing, that sought relief,
Full of wonder and full of grief,
She rolled her large bright eyes divine
Wildly on Sir Leoline.

The maid, alas! her thoughts are gone,
She nothing sees—no sight but one!
The maid, devoid of guile and sin,
I know not how, in fearful wise,
So deeply had she drunken in
That look, those shrunken serpent eyes,
That all her features were resigned
To this sole image in her mind:

And passively did imitate
That look of dull and treacherous hate!
And thus she stood, in dizzy trance,
Still picturing that look askance
With forced unconscious sympathy
Full before her father's view——
As far as such a look could be
In eyes so innocent and blue!

And when the trance was o'er, the maid
Paused awhile, and inly prayed:
Then falling at the Baron's feet,
' By my mother's soul do I entreat
That thou this woman send away!'
She said: and more she could not say:
For what she knew she could not tell,
O'er-mastered by the mighty spell.

Why is thy cheek so wan and wild,
Sir Leoline? Thy only child
Lies at thy feet, thy joy, thy pride,
So fair, so innocent, so mild;
The same, for whom thy lady died!
O, by the pangs of her dear mother
Think thou no evil of thy child!
For her, and thee, and for no other,
She prayed the moment ere she died:
Prayed that the babe for whom she died,
Might prove her dear lord's joy and pride!
    That prayer her deadly pangs beguiled,
            Sir Leoline!
    And wouldst thou wrong thy only child,
            Her child and thine?

Within the Baron's heart and brain
If thoughts, like these, had any share,
They only swelled his rage and pain,
And did but work confusion there.
His heart was cleft with pain and rage,
His cheeks they quivered, his eyes were wild,
Dishonour'd thus in his old age;
Dishonour'd by his only child,
And all his hospitality
To the insulted daughter of his friend
By more than woman's jealousy
Brought thus to a disgraceful end—
He rolled his eye with stern regard
Upon the gentle minstrel bard,
And said in tones abrupt, austere—
' Why, Bracy! dost thou loiter here?
I bade thee hence!'   The bard obeyed;
And turning from his own sweet maid,
The aged knight, Sir Leoline,
Led forth the lady Geraldine!

1801.

THE CONCLUSION TO PART THE SECOND.

A little child, a limber elf,
Singing, dancing to itself,
A fairy thing with red round cheeks,
That always finds, and never seeks,
Makes such a vision to the sight
As fills a father's eyes with light;
And pleasures flow in so thick and fast
Upon his heart, that he at last
Must needs express his love's excess
With words of unmeant bitterness.

Perhaps 'tis pretty to force together
Thoughts so all unlike each other;
To mutter and mock a broken charm,
To dally with wrong that does no harm.
Perhaps 'tis tender too and pretty
At each wild word to feel within
A sweet recoil of love and pity.
And what, if in a world of sin
(O sorrow and shame should this be true!)
Such giddiness of heart and brain
Comes seldom save from rage and pain,
So talks as it's most used to do.

? 1801.

ENCINCTURED WITH A TWINE OF LEAVES.

ENCINCTURED with a twine of leaves,
That leafy twine his only dress!
A lovely Boy was plucking fruits,
By moonlight, in a wilderness.
The moon was bright, the air was free,
And fruits and flowers together grew
On many a shrub and many a tree:
And all put on a gentle hue,
Hanging in the shadowy air
Like a picture rich and rare.
It was a climate where, they say,
The night is more belov'd than day.
But who that beauteous Boy beguil'd,
That beauteous Boy to linger here?
Alone, by night, a little child,
In place so silent and so wild—
Has he no friend, no loving mother near?

KUBLA KHAN.

In Xanadu did Kubla Khan
    A stately pleasure-dome decree:
Where Alph, the sacred river, ran
Through caverns measureless to man
    Down to a sunless sea.
So twice five miles of fertile ground
With walls and towers were girdled round:
And here were gardens bright with sinuous rills,
Where blossomed many an incense-bearing tree,
And here were forests ancient as the hills,
Enfolding sunny spots of greenery.

But oh! that deep romantic chasm which slanted
Down the green hill athwart a cedarn cover!
A savage place! as holy and enchanted
As e'er beneath a waning moon was haunted
By woman wailing for her demon-lover!
And from this chasm, with ceaseless turmoil seething,
As if this earth in fast thick pants were breathing,
A mighty fountain momently was forced,
Amid whose swift half-intermitted burst
Huge fragments vaulted like rebounding hail,
Or chaffy grain beneath the thresher's flail:
And 'mid these dancing rocks at once and ever
It flung up momently the sacred river.
Five miles meandering with a mazy motion
Through wood and dale the sacred river ran,
Then reached the caverns measureless to man,
And sank in tumult to a lifeless ocean:

And 'mid this tumult Kubla heard from far
Ancestral voices prophesying war!

    The shadow of the dome of pleasure
    Floated midway on the waves;
    Where was heard the mingled measure
    From the fountain and the caves.
It was a miracle of rare device,
A sunny pleasure-dome with caves of ice!

    A damsel with a dulcimer
    In a vision once I saw:
    It was an Abyssinian maid,
    And on her dulcimer she played,
    Singing of Mount Abora.
    Could I revive within me
    Her symphony and song,
    To such a deep delight 'twould win me,
That with music loud and long,
I would build that dome in air,
That sunny dome! those caves of ice!
And all who heard should see them there,
And all should cry, Beware! Beware!
His flashing eyes, his floating hair!
Weave a circle round him thrice,
And close your eyes with holy dread,
For he on honey-dew hath fed,
And drunk the milk of Paradise.

1797.

FABLE IS LOVE'S WORLD.

O NEVER rudely will I blame his faith
In the might of stars and angels! 'Tis not merely
The human being's Pride that peoples space
With life and mystical predominance;
Since likewise for the stricken heart of Love
This visible nature, and this common world,
Is all too narrow: yea, a deeper import
Lurks in the legend told my infant years
Than lies upon that truth, we live to learn.
For fable is Love's world, his home, his birth-place:
Delightedly dwells he 'mong fays and talismans,
And spirits; and delightedly believes
Divinities, being himself divine.
The intelligible forms of ancient poets,
The fair humanities of old religion,
The Power, the Beauty, and the Majesty,
That had her haunts in dale, or piny mountain,
Or forest by slow stream, or pebbly spring,
Or chasms and wat'ry depths; all these have vanished.
They live no longer in the faith of reason!
But still the heart doth need a language, still
Doth the old instinct bring back the old names,
And to yon starry world they now are gone,
Spirits or gods, that used to share this earth
With man as with their friend; and to the lover
Yonder they move, from yonder visible sky
Shoot influence down: and even at this day
'Tis Jupiter who brings whate'er is great,
And Venus who brings every thing that's fair.

From The Piccolomini, Schiller.

SONG

SUNG BY GLYCINE IN *ZAPOLYA*, ACT II. SCENE 2.

A SUNNY shaft did I behold,
　From sky to earth it slanted:
And poised therein a bird so bold—
　Sweet bird, thou wert enchanted!

He sunk, he rosé, he twinkled, he trolled
　Within that shaft of sunny mist;
His eyes of fire, his beak of gold,
　All else of amethyst!

And thus he sang: ' Adieu! adieu!
Love's dreams prove seldom true.
The blossoms they make no delay:
The sparkling dew-drops will not stay
　　Sweet month of May,
　　　We must away;
　　　　Far, far away!
　　　　　To-day! to-day!

1815

HUNTING SONG.

[ZAPOLYA, ACT IV. SCENE 2.]

Up, up! ye dames, and lasses gay!
To the meadows trip away.
'Tis you must tend the flocks this morn,
And scare the small birds from the corn.
 Not a soul at home may stay:
  For the shepherds must go
  With lance and bow
 To hunt the wolf in the woods to-day.

Leave the hearth and leave the house
To the cricket and the mouse:
Find grannam out a sunny seat,
With babe and lambkin at her feet.
 Not a soul at home may stay:
  For the shepherds must go
  With lance and bow
 To hunt the wolf in the woods to-day.

1815.

THE KNIGHT'S TOMB.

WHERE is the grave of Sir Arthur O'Kellyn?
Where may the grave of that good man be?—
By the side of a spring, on the breast of Helvellyn,
Under the twigs of a young birch tree!
The oak that in summer was sweet to hear,
And rustled its leaves in the fall of the year,
And whistled and roar'd in the winter alone,
Is gone,—and the birch in its stead is grown.—
The Knight's bones are dust,
And his good sword rust;—
His soul is with the saints, I trust.

? 1817.

FANCY IN NUBIBUS;

OR, THE POET IN THE CLOUDS.

O! IT is pleasant, with a heart at ease,
     Just after sunset, or by moonlight skies,
To make the shifting clouds be what you please,
     Or let the easily persuaded eyes
Own each quaint likeness issuing from the mould
     Of a friend's fancy; or with head bent low
And cheek aslant see rivers flow of gold
     'Twixt crimson banks; and then, a traveller, go
From mount to mount through Cloudland, gorgeous
          land!
     Or list'ning to the tide, with closed sight,
Be that blind bard, who on the Chian strand
     By those deep sounds possessed with inward light,
Beheld the Iliad and the Odyssee
     Rise to the swelling of the voiceful sea.

1819.

CATULLIAN HENDECASYLLABLES.

Hear, my beloved, an old Milesian story!—
High, and embosom'd in congregated laurels,
Glimmer'd a temple upon a breezy headland;
In the dim distance amid the skiey billows
Rose a fair island; the god of flocks had blest it.
From the far shores of the bleat-resounding island
Oft by the moonlight a little boat came floating,
Came to the sea-cave beneath the breezy headland,
Where amid myrtles a pathway stole in mazes
Up to the groves of the high embosom'd temple.
There in a thicket of dedicated roses,
Oft did a priestess, as lovely as a vision,
Pouring her soul to the son of Cytherea,
Pray him to hover around the slight canoe-boat,
And with invisible pilotage to guide it
Over the dusk wave, until the nightly sailor
Shivering with ecstasy sank upon her bosom.

$\}$ 1799.

TIME, REAL AND IMAGINARY

AN ALLEGORY.

On the wide level of a mountain's head,
(I knew not where, but 'twas some faery place)
Their pinions, ostrich-like, for sails outspread,
Two lovely children run an endless race,
    A sister and a brother!
    This far outstript the other;
  Yet ever runs she with reverted face,
And looks and listens for the boy behind:
    For he, alas! is blind!
O'er rough and smooth with even step he passed,
And knows not whether he be first or last.

YOUTH AND AGE.

Verse, a breeze mid blossoms straying,
Where Hope clung feeding, like a bee—
Both were mine!   Life went a-maying
        With Nature, Hope, and Poesy,
           When I was young!

When I was young?—Ah, woful When!
Ah! for the change 'twixt Now and Then!
This breathing house not built with hands,
This body that does me grievous wrong,
O'er aery cliffs and glittering sands,
How lightly *then* it flashed along:—
Like those trim skiffs, unknown of yore,
On winding lakes and rivers wide,
That ask no aid of sail or oar,
That fear no spite of wind or tide!
Nought cared this body for wind or weather
When Youth and I lived in't together.

Flowers are lovely; Love is flower-like;
Friendship is a sheltering tree;
O! the joys, that came down shower-like,
Of Friendship, Love, and Liberty,
           Ere I was old!

Ere I was old?   Ah woful Ere,
Which tells me, Youth's no longer here!
O Youth! for years so many and sweet,
'Tis known, that Thou and I were one,

I'll think it but a fond conceit—
It cannot be that Thou art gone!
Thy vesper-bell hath not yet toll'd:—
And thou wert aye a masker bold!
What strange disguise hast now put on,
To *make believe*, that thou art gone?
I see these locks in silvery slips,
This drooping gait, this altered size:
But Spring-tide blossoms on thy lips,
And tears take sunshine from thine eyes!
Life is but thought: so think I will
That Youth and I are house-mates still.

Dew-drops are the gems of morning,
But the tears of mournful eve!
Where no hope is, life's a warning
That only serves to make us grieve,
                              When we are old:
That only serves to make us grieve
With oft and tedious taking-leave,
Like some poor nigh-related guest,
That may not rudely be dismist;
Yet hath outstay'd his welcome while,
And tells the jest without the smile.

1822-1832.

IV.

LOVE POEMS.

LOVE.

ALL thoughts, all passions, all delights,
Whatever stirs this mortal frame,
All are but ministers of Love,
    And feed his sacred flame.

Oft in my waking dreams do I
Live o'er again that happy hour,
When midway on the mount I lay,
    Beside the ruined tower.

The moonshine, stealing o'er the scene
Had blended with the lights of eve;
And she was there, my hope, my joy,
    My own dear Genevieve!

She leant against the armed man,
The statue of the armed knight;
She stood and listened to my lay,
    Amid the lingering light.

Few sorrows hath she of her own.
My hope! my joy! my Genevieve!
She loves me best, whene'er I sing
    The songs that make her grieve.

I played a soft and doleful air,
I sang an old and moving story—
An old rude song, that suited well
    That ruin wild and hoary.

She listened with a flitting blush,
With downcast eyes and modest grace;
For well she knew, I could not choose
    But gaze upon her face.

I told her of the knight that wore
Upon his shield a burning brand;
And that for ten long years he wooed
    The Lady of the Land.

I told her how he pined: and ah!
The deep, the low, the pleading tone
With which I sang another's love,
    Interpreted my own.

She listened with a flitting blush,
With downcast eyes, and modest grace
And she forgave me, that I gazed
    Too fondly on her face!

But when I told the cruel scorn
That crazed that bold and lovely Knight,
And that he crossed the mountain-woods,
    Nor rested day nor night;

That sometimes from the savage den,
And sometimes from the darksome shade
And sometimes starting up at once
    In green and sunny glade,—

There came and looked him in the face
An angel beautiful and bright;
And that he knew it was a Fiend,
    This miserable Knight!

And that unknowing what he did,
He leaped amid a murderous band,
And saved from outrage worse than death
    The Lady of the Land!

And how she wept, and clasped his knees;
And how she tended him in vain—
And ever strove to expiate
    The scorn that crazed his brain;—

And that she nursed him in a cave;
And how his madness went away,
When on the yellow forest-leaves
    A dying man he lay;—

His dying words—but when I reached
That tenderest strain of all the ditty,
My faltering voice and pausing harp
    Disturbed her soul with pity!

All impulses of soul and sense
Had thrilled my guileless Genevieve;
The music and the doleful tale,
    The rich and balmy eve;

And hopes, and fears that kindle hope,
An undistinguishable throng,
And gentle wishes long subdued,
    Subdued and cherished long!

She wept with pity and delight,
She blushed with love, and virgin-shame;
And like the murmur of a dream,
    I heard her breathe my name.

Her bosom heaved—she stepped aside,
As conscious of my look she stepped—
Then suddenly, with timorous eye
    She fled to me and wept.

She half enclosed me with her arms,
She pressed me with a meek embrace;
And bending back her head, looked up,
    And gazed upon my face.

'Twas partly love, and partly fear,
And partly 'twas a bashful art,
That I might rather feel, than see,
    The swelling of her heart.

I calmed her fears, and she was calm,
And told her love with virgin pride;
And so I won my Genevieve,
    My bright and beauteous Bride.

                    1798-1799.

WESTPHALIAN SONG.

When thou to my true-love com'st
    Greet her from me kindly;
When she asks thee how I fare?
    Say, folks in Heaven fare finely.

When she asks, 'What! Is he sick?'
    Say, dead!—and when for sorrow
She begins to sob and cry,
    Say, I come to-morrow.

                    ? 1799.

LEWTI;

OR THE CIRCASSIAN LOVE-CHAUNT.

At midnight by the stream I roved,
To forget the form I loved.
Image of Lewti! from my mind
Depart; for Lewti is not kind.

The Moon was high, the moon-light gleam
   And the shadow of a star
Heaved upon Tamaha's stream;
   But the rock shone brighter far,
The rock half sheltered from my view
By pendent boughs of tressy yew.—
So shines my Lewti's forehead fair,
Gleaming through her sable hair,
Image of Lewti! from my mind
Depart; for Lewti is not kind.

I saw a cloud of palest hue,
   Onward to the moon it passed;
Still brighter and more bright it grew,
With floating colours not a few,
   Till it reach'd the moon at last:
Then the cloud was wholly bright,
With a rich and amber light!

And so with many a hope I seek
   And with such joy I find my Lewti;
And even so my pale wan cheek
   Drinks in as deep a flush of beauty!
Nay, treacherous image! leave my mind,
If Lewti never will be kind.

The little cloud—it floats away,
   Away it goes; away so soon?
Alas! it has no power to stay:
Its hues are dim, its hues are grey
   Away it passes from the moon!
How mournfully it seems to fly,
   Ever fading more and more,
To joyless regions of the sky—
   And now 'tis whiter than before!
As white as my poor cheek will be,
   When, Lewti! on my couch I lie,
A dying man for love of thee.
Nay, treacherous image! leave my mind—
And yet, thou didst not look unkind.

I saw a vapour in the sky,
   Thin, and white, and very high;
I ne'er beheld so thin a cloud:
   Perhaps the breezes that can fly
   Now below and now above,
Have snatched aloft the lawny shroud
   Of Lady fair—that died for love.
For maids, as well as youths, have perished
From fruitless love too fondly cherished.
Nay, treacherous image! leave my mind—
For Lewti never will be kind.

Hush! my heedless feet from under
  Slip the crumbling banks for ever:
Like echoes to a distant thunder,
  They plunge into the gentle river.
The river-swans have heard my tread,
And startle from their reedy bed.
O beauteous birds! methinks ye measure
  Your movements to some heavenly tune!
O beauteous birds! 'tis such a pleasure
  To see you move beneath the moon,
I would it were your true delight
To sleep by day and wake all night.

I know the place where Lewti lies
When silent night has closed her eyes:
  It is a breezy jasmine-bower,
The nightingale sings o'er her head:
  Voice of the Night! had I the power
That leafy labyrinth to thread,
And creep, like thee, with soundless tread,
I then might view her bosom white
Heaving lovely to my sight,
As these two swans together heave
On the gently-swelling wave.

Oh! that she saw me in a dream,
  And dreamt that I had died for care;
All pale and wasted I would seem
  Yet fair withal, as spirits are!
I'd die indeed, if I might see
Her bosom heave, and heave for me!
Soothe, gentle image! soothe my mind!
To-morrow Lewti may be kind.

1794.

THE SNOW-DROP.

[A FRAGMENT.]

I.

FEAR thou no more, thou timid Flower!
Fear thou no more the winter's might,
The whelming thaw, the ponderous shower,
The silence of the freezing night!
Since Laura murmur'd o'er thy leaves
The potent sorceries of song,
To thee, meek Flowret! gentler gales
    And cloudless skies belong.

.   .   .   .

III.

She droop'd her head, she stretch'd her arm,
She whisper'd low her witching rhymes,
Fame unreluctant heard the charm,
And bore thee to Pierian climes!
Fear thou no more the Matin Frost
That sparkled on thy bed of snow:
For there, mid laurels ever green,
    Immortal thou shalt blow.

IV.

Thy petals boast a white more soft,
The spell hath so perfumed thee,
That careless Love shall deem thee oft
A blossom from his Myrtle tree.

Then laughing o'er the fair deceit
Shall race with some Etesian wind
To seek the woven arboret
    Where Laura lies reclin'd.

v.

All them whom Love and Fancy grace,
When grosser eyes are clos'd in sleep,
The gentle spirits of the place
Waft up the insuperable steep,
On whose vast summit broad and smooth
Her nest the Phœnix Bird conceals,
And where by cypresses o'erhung
    The heavenly Lethe steals.

vi.

A sea-like sound the branches breathe,
Stirr'd by the Breeze that loiters there;
And all that stretch their limbs beneath,
Forget the coil of mortal care.
Strange mists along the margins rise,
To heal the guests who thither come,
And fit the soul to re-endure
    Its earthly martyrdom.

MS.   ? 1800.

RECOLLECTIONS OF LOVE

I.

How warm this woodland wild recess!
  Love surely hath been breathing here:
  And this sweet bed of heath, my dear!
Swells up, then sinks with fair caress,
  As if to have you yet more near.

II.

Eight springs have flown, since last I lay
  On sea-ward Quantock's heathy hills,
  Where quiet sounds from hidden rills
Float here and there, like things astray,
  And high o'er head the sky-lark shrills.

III.

No voice as yet had made the air
  Be music with your name; yet why
  That asking look? that yearning sigh?
That sense of promise every where?
  Beloved! flew your spirit by?

1803-1807.

A DAY-DREAM.

My eyes make pictures, when they are shut:
    I see a fountain, large and fair,
A willow and a ruined hut,
    And thee, and me and Mary there.
O Mary! make thy gentle lap our pillow!
Bend o'er us, like a bower, my beautiful green willow!

A wild-rose roofs the ruined shed,
    And that and summer well agree:
And lo! where Mary leans her head,
    Two dear names carved upon the tree!
And Mary's tears, they are not tears of sorrow:
Our sister and our friend will both be here to-morrow.

'Twas day! but now few, large, and bright,
    The stars are round the crescent moon!
And now it is a dark warm night,
    The balmiest of the month of June!
A glow-worm fall'n, and on the marge remounting
Shines, and its shadow shines, fit stars for our sweet
       fountain.

O ever—ever be thou blest!
    For dearly, Asra! love I thee!
This brooding warmth across my breast,
    This depth of tranquil bliss—ah, me!
Fount, tree and shed are gone, I know not whither,
But in one quiet room we three are still together.

The shadows dance upon the wall,
　　By the still dancing fire-flames made;
And now they slumber moveless all!
　　　And now they melt to one deep shade!
But not from me shall this mild darkness steal thee:
I dream thee with mine eyes, and at my heart I feel t

　　　　　　　　　　　? 1807.

MUTUAL PASSION.

ALTERED AND MODERNIZED FROM AN OLD POET.

I LOVE, and he loves me again,
　　Yet dare I not tell who:
For if the nymphs should know my swain,
　　I fear they'd love him too.
　　　Yet while my joy's unknown,
　　　Its rosy buds are but half-blown:
What no one with me shares, seems scarce my own.

I'll tell, that if they be not glad,
　　They yet may envy me:
But then if I grow jealous mad,
　　And of them pitied be,
　　　'Twould vex me worse than scorn!
　　　And yet it cannot be forborne,
Unless my heart would like my thoughts be torn.

He is, if they can find him, fair
　　And fresh, and fragrant too;
As after rain the summer air,
　　And looks as lilies do,

That are this morning blown!
Yet, yet I doubt, he is not known,
Yet, yet I fear to have him fully shown.

But he hath eyes so large, and bright,
    Which none can see, and doubt
That Love might thence his torches light
    Tho' Hate had put them out!
        But then to raise my fears,
        His voice——what maid so ever hears
Will be my rival, though she have but ears.

I'll tell no more! yet I love him,
    And he loves me; yet so,
That never one low wish did dim
    Our love's pure light, I know——
        In each so free from blame,
        That both of us would gain new fame,
If love's strong fears would let me tell his name!

? 1799.

THEKLA'S SONG

FROM SCHILLER.

THE cloud doth gather, the greenwood roar,
The damsel paces along the shore;
The billows they tumble with might, with might;
And she flings out her voice to the darksome night;
     Her bosom is swelling with sorrow;
The world it is empty, the heart will die,
There's nothing to wish for beneath the sky:
Thou Holy One, call Thy child away!
I've lived and loved, and that was to-day—
     Make ready my grave-clothes to-morrow.

LOVE'S FIRST HOPE.

O FAIR is Love's first hope to gentle mind!
As Eve's first star thro' fleecy cloudlet peeping;
And sweeter than the gentle south-west wind,
O'er willowy meads, and shadow'd waters creeping,
And Ceres' golden fields; the sultry hind
Meets it with brow uplift, and stays his reaping.

WATER BALLAD.

' Come hither, gently rowing,
  Come, bear me quickly o'er
This stream so brightly flowing
  To yonder woodland shore.
But vain were my endeavour
  To pay thee, courteous guide;
Row on, row on, for ever
  I'd have thee by my side.

' Good boatman, prithee haste thee,
  I seek my father-land.'—
' Say, when I there have placed thee,
  Dare I demand thy hand?'
' A maiden's head can never
  So hard a point decide;
Row on, row on, for ever
  I'd have thee by my side.'

The happy bridal over
  The wanderer ceased to roam,
For, seated by her lover,
  The boat became her home.
And still they sang together
  As steering o'er the tide:
' Row on through wind and weather
  For ever by my side.'

                              ? 1799.

MORIENS SUPERSTITI.

THE hour-bell sounds, and I must go;
Death waits—again I hear him calling;—
No cowardly desires have I,
Nor will I shun his face appalling.
I die in faith and honour rich—
But ah! I leave behind my treasure
In widowhood and lonely pain;—
To live were surely then a pleasure!

My lifeless eyes upon thy face
Shall never open more to-morrow;
To-morrow shall thy beauteous eyes
Be closed to love, and drown'd in sorrow;
To-morrow death shall freeze this hand,
And on thy breast, my wedded treasure,
I never, never more shall live;—
Alas! I quit a life of pleasure.
                    Morning Post, May 10, 1798.

MORIENTI SUPERSTES.

YET art thou happier far than she
Who feels the widow's love for thee!
For while her days are days of weeping,
Thou, in peace, in silence sleeping,
In some still world, unknown, remote,
    The mighty parent's care hast found,
Without whose tender guardian thought
    No sparrow falleth to the ground.

THE KEEPSAKE.

THE tedded hay, the first fruits of the soil,
The tedded hay and corn-sheaves in one field,
Show summer gone, ere come. The foxglove tall
Sheds its loose purple bells, or in the gust,
Or when it bends beneath the up-springing lark,
Or mountain-finch alighting. And the rose
(In vain the darling of successful love)
Stands, like some boasted beauty of past years,
The thorns remaining, and the flowers all gone.
Nor can I find, amid my lonely walk
By rivulet, or spring, or wet road-side,
That blue and bright-eyed floweret of the brook,
Hope's gentle gem, the sweet Forget-me-not!
So will not fade the flowers which Emmeline
With delicate fingers on the snow-white silk
Has worked (the flowers which most she knew I
    loved),
And, more beloved than they, her auburn hair.

In the cool morning twilight, early waked
By her full bosom's joyous restlessness,
Softly she rose, and lightly stole along,
Down the slope coppice to the woodbine bower,
Whose rich flowers, swinging in the morning breeze,
Over their dim fast-moving shadows hung,
Making a quiet image of disquiet
In the smooth, scarcely moving river-pool.

There, in that bower where first she owned her love,
And let me kiss my own warm tear of joy
From off her glowing cheek, she sate and stretched
The silk upon the frame, and worked her name
Between the Moss-Rose and Forget-me-not—
Her own dear name, with her own auburn hair!
That forced to wander till sweet spring return,
I yet might ne'er forget her smile, her look,
Her voice (that even in her mirthful mood
Has made me wish to steal away and weep),
Nor yet the entrancement of that maiden kiss
With which she promised, that when spring returned,
She would resign one half of that dear name,
And own thenceforth no other name but mine!

1800.

THE PICTURE

OR THE LOVER'S RESOLUTION.

THROUGH weeds and thorns, and matted underwood
I force my way; now climb, and now descend
O'er rocks, or bare or mossy, with wild foot
Crushing the purple whorts; while oft unseen,
Hurrying along the drifted forest-leaves,
The scared snake rustles. Onward still I toil,
I know not, ask not whither! A new joy,
Lovely as light, sudden as summer gust,
And gladsome as the first-born of the spring,
Beckons me on, or follows from behind,
Playmate, or guide! The master-passion quelled,
I feel that I am free. With dun-red bark
The fir-trees, and the unfrequent slender oak,
Forth from this tangle wild of bush and brake
Soar up, and form a melancholy vault
High o'er me, murmuring like a distant sea.

Here Wisdom might resort, and here Remorse;
Here too the love-lorn man, who, sick in soul,
And of this busy human heart aweary,
Worships the spirit of unconscious life
In tree or wild-flower.—Gentle lunatic!
If so he might not wholly cease to be,

He would far rather not be that he is;
But would be something that he knows not of,
In winds or waters, or among the rocks!

But hence, fond wretch! breathe not contagion
    here!
No myrtle-walks are these: these are no groves
Where Love dare loiter! If in sullen mood
He should stray hither, the low stumps shall gore
His dainty feet, the briar and the thorn
Make his plumes haggard. Like a wounded bird
Easily caught, ensnare him, O ye Nymphs,
Ye Oreads chaste, ye dusky Dryades!
And you, ye Earth-winds! you that make at morn
The dew-drops quiver on the spiders' webs!
You, O ye wingless Airs! that creep between
The rigid stems of heath and bitten furze,
Within whose scanty shade, at summer-noon,
The mother-sheep hath worn a hollow bed—
Ye, that now cool her fleece with dropless damp,
Now pant and murmur with her feeding lamb.
Chase, chase him, all ye Fays, and elfin Gnomes!
With prickles sharper than his darts bemock
His little Godship, making him perforce
Creep through a thorn-bush on yon hedgehog's
    back.

This is my hour of triumph! I can now
With my own fancies play the merry fool,
And laugh away worse folly, being free.
Here will I seat myself, beside this old,
Hollow, and weedy oak, which ivy twine
Clothes as with net-work: here will couch my
    limbs,

Close by this river, in this silent shade,
As safe and sacred from the step of man
As an invisible world—unheard, unseen,
And listening only to the pebbly brook
That murmurs with a dead, yet tinkling sound;
Or to the bees, that in the neighbouring trunk
Make honey-hoards. The breeze, that visits me,
Was never Love's accomplice, never raised
The tendril ringlets from the maiden's brow,
And the blue, delicate veins above her cheek;
Ne'er played the wanton—never half disclosed
The maiden's snowy bosom, scattering thence
Eye-poisons for some love-distempered youth,
Who ne'er henceforth may see an aspen-grove
Shiver in sunshine, but his feeble heart
Shall flow away like a dissolving thing.

Sweet breeze! thou only, if I guess aright,
Liftest the feathers of the robin's breast,
That swells its little breast, so full of song,
Singing above me, on the mountain-ash.
And thou too, desert stream! no pool of thine,
Though clear as lake in latest summer-eve,
Did e'er reflect the stately virgin's robe,
The face, the form divine, the downcast look
Contemplative! Behold! her open palm
Presses her cheek and brow! her elbow rests
On the bare branch of half-uprooted tree,
That leans towards its mirror! Who erewhile
Had from her countenance turned, or looked by
      stealth
(For fear is true-love's cruel nurse), he now
With steadfast gaze and unoffending eye,
Worships the watery idol, dreaming hopes

Delicious to the soul, but fleeting, vain,
E'en as that phantom world on which he gazed,
But not unheeded gazed: for see, ah! see,
The sportive tyrant with her left hand plucks
The heads of tall flowers that behind her grow,
Lychnis, and willow-herb, and fox-glove bells:
And suddenly, as one that toys with time,
Scatters them on the pool! Then all the charm
Is broken—all that phantom world so fair
Vanishes, and a thousand circlets spread,
And each mis-shapes the other. Stay awhile,
Poor youth, who scarcely dar'st lift up thine eyes!
The stream will soon renew its smoothness, soon
The visions will return! And lo! he stays:
And soon the fragments dim of lovely forms
Come trembling back, unite, and now once more
The pool becomes a mirror; and behold
Each wildflower on the marge inverted there,
And there the half-uprooted tree—but where,
O where the virgin's snowy arm, that leaned
On its bare branch? He turns, and she is gone!
Homeward she steals through many a woodland
        maze
Which he shall seek in vain. I'll-fated youth!
Go, day by day, and waste thy manly prime
In mad love-yearning by the vacant brook,
Till sickly thoughts bewitch thine eyes, and thou
Behold'st her shadow still abiding there,
The Naiad of the mirror!

                              Not to thee,
O wild and desert stream! belongs this tale:
Gloomy and dark art thou—the crowded firs
Spire from thy shores, and stretch across thy bed,
Making thee doleful as a cavern-well:

Save when the shy king-fishers build their nest
On thy steep banks, no loves hast thou, wild
    stream!

  This be my chosen haunt—emancipate
From passion's dreams, a freeman, and alone,
I rise and trace its devious course. O lead,
Lead me to deeper shades and lonelier glooms.
Lo! stealing through the canopy of firs,
How fair the sunshine spots that mossy rock,
Isle of the river, whose disparted waves
Dart off asunder with an angry sound,
How soon to re-unite! And see! they meet,
Each in the other lost and found: and see
Placeless, as spirits, one soft water-sun
Throbbing within them, heart at once and eye!
With its soft neighbourhood of filmy clouds,
The stains and shadings of forgotten tears,
Dimness o'erswum with lustre! Such the hour
Of deep enjoyment, following love's brief feuds;
And hark, the noise of a near waterfall!
I pass forth into light—I find myself
Beneath a weeping birch (most beautiful
Of forest trees, the Lady of the Woods),
Hard by the brink of a tall weedy rock
That overbrows the cataract. How bursts
The landscape on my sight! Two crescent hills
Fold in behind each other, and so make
A circular vale, and land-locked, as might seem,
With brook and bridge, and grey stone cottages,
Half hid by rocks and fruit-trees. At my feet,
The whortle-berries are bedewed with spray,
Dashed upwards by the furious waterfall.
How solemnly the pendent ivy-mass

Swings in its winnow: All the air is calm.
The smoke from cottage-chimneys, tinged with
    light,
Rises in columns; from this house alone,
Close by the waterfall, the column slants,
And feels its ceaseless breeze. But what is this?
That cottage, with its slanting chimney-smoke,
And close beside its porch a sleeping child,
His dear head pillow'd on a sleeping dog—
One arm between its fore-legs, and the hand
Holds loosely its small handful of wild-flowers,
Unfilleted, and of unequal lengths.
A curious picture, with a master's haste
Sketched on a strip of pinky-silver skin,
Peeled from the birchen bark! Divinest maid!
Yon bark her canvas, and those purple berries
Her pencil! See, the juice is scarcely dried
On the fine skin! She has been newly here;
And lo! yon patch of heath has been her couch—
The pressure still remains! O blessed couch!
For this may'st thou flower early, and the sun,
Slanting at eve, rest bright, and linger long
Upon thy purple bells! O Isabel!
Daughter of genius! stateliest of our maids!
More beautiful than whom Alcæus wooed,
The Lesbian woman of immortal song!
O child of genius! stately, beautiful,
And full of love to all, save only me,
And not ungentle e'en to me! My heart,
Why beats it thus? Through yonder coppice-wood
Needs must the pathway turn, that leads straight-
    way
On to her father's house. She is alone!
The night draws on—such ways are hard to hit—

And fit it is I should restore this sketch,
Dropt unawares no doubt.   Why should I yearn
To keep the relique? 'twill but idly feed
The passion that consumes me.   Let me haste!
The picture in my hand which she has left;
She cannot blame me that I follow'd her:
And I may be her guide the long wood through.

1802.

TO LESBIA.

"Vivamus, mea Lesbia, atque amemus."
CATULLUS.

My Lesbia, let us love and live,
And to the winds, my Lesbia, give
Each cold restraint, each boding fear
Of age and all her saws severe.
Yon sun now posting to the main
Will set,—but 'tis to rise again;—
But we, when once our mortal light
Is set, must sleep in endless night.
Then come, with whom alone I'll live,
A thousand kisses take and give!
Another thousand!—to the store
Add hundreds—then a thousand more!
And when they to a million mount,
Let confusion take the account,—
That you, the number never knowing,
May continue still bestowing—
That I for joys may never pine,
Which never can again be mine!

Morning Post, April 11, 1798.

NAMES.

[FROM LESSING.]

I ASK'D my fair one happy day,
What I should call her in my lay;
  By what sweet name from Rome or Greece;
Lalage, Neæra, Chloris,
Sappho, Lesbia, or Doris,
  Arethusa or Lucrece.

'Ah!' replied my gentle fair,
'Beloved, what are names but air?
  Choose thou whatever suits the line;
Call me Sappho, call me Chloris,
Call me Lalage or Doris,
  Only, only call me Thine.'

Morning Post, August 27, 1799.

V.
NARRATIVE AND OCCASIONAL POEMS

THE THREE GRAVES.

A FRAGMENT OF A SEXTON'S TALE.

PART III.

The grapes upon the Vicar's wall
   Were ripe as ripe could be;
And yellow leaves in sun and wind
   Were falling from the tree.

On the hedge-elms in the narrow lane
   Still swung the spikes of corn:
Dear Lord! it seems but yesterday—
   Young Edward's marriage-morn.

Up through that wood behind the church,
   There leads from Edward's door
A mossy track, all over boughed,
   For half a mile or more.

And from their house-door by that track
   The bride and bridegroom went;
Sweet Mary, though she was not gay,
   Seemed cheerful and content.

But when they to the church-yard came,
   I've heard poor Mary say,
As soon as she stepped into the sun,
   Her heart it died away.

And when the Vicar join'd their hands,
    Her limbs did creep and freeze;
But when they prayed, she thought she saw
    Her mother on her knees.

And o'er the church-path they returned—
    I saw poor Mary's back,
Just as she stepped beneath the boughs
    Into the mossy track.

Her feet upon the mossy track
    The married maiden set:
That moment—I have heard her say—
    She wished she could forget.

The shade o'er-flushed her limbs with heat—
    Then came a chill like death:
And when the merry bells rang out,
    They seemed to stop her breath.

Beneath the foulest mother's curse
    No child could ever thrive:
A mother is a mother still,
    The holiest thing alive.

So five months passed: the mother still
    Would never heal the strife;
But Edward was a loving man,
    And Mary a fond wife.

' My sister may not visit us,
    My mother says her nay:
O Edward! you are all to me,
I wish for your sake I could be
    More lifesome and more gay.

' I'm dull and sad! Indeed, indeed
   I know I have no reason!
Perhaps I am not well in health,
   And 'tis a gloomy season.'

'Twas a drizzly time—no ice, no snow!
   And on the few fine days
She stirred not out, lest she might meet
   Her mother in the ways.

But Ellen, spite of miry ways
   And weather dark and dreary,
Trudged every day to Edward's house,
   And made them all more cheery.

Oh! Ellen was a faithful friend,
   More dear than any sister!
As cheerful too as singing lark;
   And she ne'er left them till 'twas dark,
   And then they always missed her.

And now Ash-Wednesday came—that day
   But few to church repair:
For on that day you know we read
   The Commination prayer.

Our late old Vicar, a kind man,
   Once, Sir, he said to me,
He wished that service was clean out
   Of our good Liturgy.

The mother walked into the church—
   To Ellen's seat she went:
Though Ellen always kept her church
   All church-days during Lent.

And gentle Ellen welcomed her
  With courteous looks and mild:
Thought she, 'What if her heart should melt,
  And all be reconciled!'

The day was scarcely like a day—
  The clouds were black outright:
And many a night, with half a moon
  I've seen the church more light.

The wind was wild; against the glass
  The rain did beat and bicker;
The church-tower swinging over head,
  You scarce could hear the Vicar!

And then and there the mother knelt,
  And audibly she cried—
'Oh! may a clinging curse consume
  This woman by my side!

'O hear me, hear me, Lord in Heaven,
  Although you take my life—
O curse this woman, at whose house
  Young Edward woo'd his wife.

'By night and day, in bed and bower,
  O let her cursed be! ! !'
So having prayed, steady and slow,
  She rose up from her knee!
And left the church, nor e'er again
  The church-door entered she.

I saw poor Ellen kneeling still,
  So pale! I guessed not why:
When she stood up, there plainly was
  A trouble in her eye.

And when the prayers were done, we all
   Came round and asked her why:
Giddy she seemed, and sure, there was
   A trouble in her eye.

But ere she from the church-door stepped
   She smiled and told us why:
' It was a wicked woman's curse,'
   Quoth she, ' and what care I ? '

She smiled, and smiled, and passed it off
   Ere from the door she stept—
But all agree it would have been
   Much better had she wept.

And if her heart was not at ease,
   This was her constant cry—
' It was a wicked woman's curse—
   God's good, and what care I ? '

There was a hurry in her looks,
   Her struggles she redoubled:
' It was a wicked woman's curse,
   And why should I be troubled ? '

These tears will come—I dandled her
   When 'twas the merest fairy—
Good creature! and she hid it all:
   She told it not to Mary.

But Mary heard the tale: her arms
   Round Ellen's neck she threw;
' O Ellen, Ellen, she cursed me,
   And now she hath cursed you ! '

I saw young Edward by himself
   Stalk fast adown the lee,
He snatched a stick from every fence,
   A twig from every tree.

He snapped them still with hand or knee,
   And then away they flew!
As if with his uneasy limbs
   He knew not what to do!

You see, good sir! that single hill?
   His farm lies underneath:
He heard it there, he heard it all,
   And only gnashed his teeth.

Now Ellen was a darling love
   In all his joys and cares:
And Ellen's name and Mary's name
Fast-linked they both together came,
   Whene'er he said his prayers.

And in the moment of his prayers
   He loved them both alike:
Yea, both sweet names with one sweet joy
   Upon his heart did strike!

He reach'd his home, and by his looks
   They saw his inward strife:
And they clung round him with their arms,
   Both Ellen and his wife.

And Mary could not check her tears,
   So on his breast she bowed;
Then frenzy melted into grief,
   And Edward wept aloud.

Dear Ellen did not weep at all,
   But closelier did she cling,
And turned her face and looked as if
   She saw some frightful thing.

PART IV.

To see a man tread over graves
   I hold it no good mark;
'Tis wicked in the sun and moon,
   And bad luck in the dark!

You see that grave?   The Lord he gives,
   The Lord, he takes away:
O Sir! the child of my old age
   Lies there as cold as clay.

Except that grave, you scarce see one
   That was not dug by me;
I'd rather dance upon 'em all
   Than tread upon these three!

' Aye, Sexton! 'tis a touching tale.'
   You, Sir! are but a lad;
This month I'm in my seventieth year,
   And still it makes me sad.

And Mary's sister told it me,
   For three good hours and more;
'Though I had heard it, in the main,
   From Edward's self, before.

Well! it passed off! the gentle Ellen
    Did well nigh dote on Mary;
And she went oftener than before,
And Mary loved her more and more:
    She managed all the dairy.

To market she on market-days,
    To church on Sundays came;
All seemed the same: all seemed so, Sir!
    But all was not the same!

Had Ellen lost her mirth? Oh! no!
    But she was seldom cheerful;
And Edward look'd as if he thought
    That Ellen's mirth was fearful.

When by herself, she to herself
    Must sing some merry rhyme;
She could not now be glad for hours,
    Yet silent all the time.

And when she soothed her friend, through all
    Her soothing words 'twas plain
She had a sore grief of her own,
    A haunting in her brain.

And oft she said, I'm not grown thin!
    And then her wrist she spanned;
And once when Mary was down-cast,
    She took her by the hand,
And gazed upon her, and at first
    She gently pressed her hand;

Then harder, till her grasp at length
　　Did gripe like a convulsion!
'Alas!' said she, 'we ne'er can be
　　Made happy by compulsion!'

And once her both arms suddenly
　　Round Mary's neck she flung,
And her heart panted, and she felt
　　The words upon her tongue.

She felt them coming, but no power
　　Had she the words to smother;
And with a kind of shriek she cried,
　　'Oh Christ! you're like your mother!'

So gentle Ellen now no more
　　Could make this sad house cheery;
And Mary's melancholy ways
　　Drove Edward wild and weary.

Lingering he raised his latch at eve,
　　Though tired in heart and limb:
He loved no other place, and yet
　　Home was no home to him.

One evening he took up a book,
　　And nothing in it read;
Then flung it down, and groaning cried,
　　'O! Heaven! that I were dead.'

Mary looked up into his face,
　　And nothing to him said;
She tried to smile, and on his arm
　　Mournfully leaned her head.

And he burst into tears, and fell
    Upon his knees in prayer:
' Her heart is broke! O God! my grief,
    It is too great to bear!'

'Twas such a foggy time as makes
    Old sextons, Sir! like me,
Rest on their spades to cough; the spring
    Was late uncommonly.

And then the hot days, all at once,
    They came, we knew not how:
You looked about for shade, when scarce
    A leaf was on a bough.

It happened then ('twas in the bower,
    A furlong up the wood:
Perhaps you know the place, and yet
    I scarce know how you should,)

No path leads thither, 'tis not nigh
    To any pasture-plot;
But clustered near the chattering brook,
    Lone hollies marked the spot.

Those hollies of themselves a shape
    As of an arbour took,
A close, round arbour; and it stands
    Not three strides from a brook.

Within this arbour, which was still
    With scarlet berries hung,
Were these three friends, one Sunday morn,
    Just as the first bell rung.

'Tis sweet to hear a brook, 'tis sweet
    To hear the Sabbath-bell,
'Tis sweet to hear them both at once,
    Deep in a woody dell.

His limbs along the moss, his head
    Upon a mossy heap,
With shut-up senses, Edward lay:
That brook e'en on a working day
    Might chatter one to sleep.

And he had passed a restless night,
    And was not well in health;
The women sat down by his side,
    And talked as 'twere by stealth.

' The Sun peeps through the close thick leaves,
    See, dearest Ellen! see!
'Tis in the leaves, a little sun,
    No bigger than your ee;

' A tiny sun, and it has got
    A perfect glory too;
Ten thousand threads and hairs of light,
Make up a glory gay and bright
    Round that small orb, so blue.'

And then they argued of those rays,
    What colour they might be;
Says this, ' They're mostly green ' ; says that,
    ' They're amber-like to me.'

So they sat chatting, while bad thoughts
    Were troubling Edward's rest;
But soon they heard his hard quick pants,
    And the thumping in his breast.

'A mother too!' these self-same words
    Did Edward mutter plain;
His face was drawn back on itself,
    With horror and huge pain.

Both groan'd at once, for both knew well
    What thoughts were in his mind;
When he waked up, and stared like one
    That hath been just struck blind.

He sat upright; and ere the dream
    Had had time to depart,
'O God, forgive me!' (he exclaimed)
    'I have torn out her heart.'

Then Ellen shrieked, and forthwith burst
    Into ungentle laughter;
And Mary shivered, where she sat,
    And never she smiled after.

                                    1797-1809

THE BALLAD OF THE DARK LADIE.

A FRAGMENT.

O LEAVE the lily on its stem;
O leave the rose upon the spray;
O leave the elder-bloom, fair maids!
    And listen to my lay.

A cypress and a myrtle bough
This morn around my harp you twined,
Because it fashion'd mournfully
    Its murmurs in the wind.

And now a tale of love and woe,
A woeful tale of love I sing;
Hark, gentle maidens! hark, it sighs
    And trembles on the string.

But most, my own dear Genevieve,
It sighs and trembles most for thee!
O come and hear the cruel wrongs,
    Befel the dark Ladie!

.   .   .   .   .

Beneath yon birch with silver bark,
And boughs so pendulous and fair,
The brook falls scatter'd down the rock
    And all is mossy there!

And there upon the moss she sits,
The Dark Ladié in silent pain;
The heavy tear is in her eye,
 And drops and swells again.

Three times she sends her little page
Up the castled mountain's breast,
If he might find the Knight that wears
 The Griffin for his crest.

The sun was sloping down the sky,
And she had linger'd there all day,
Counting moments, dreaming fears—
 Oh wherefore can he stay?

She hears a rustling o'er the brook,
She sees far off a swinging bough?
' 'Tis He! 'Tis my betrothed Knight!
 Lord Falkland, it is Thou!'

She springs, she clasps him round the neck,
She sobs a thousand hopes and fears,
Her kisses glowing on his cheeks
 She quenches with her tears.

. . . . . .

' My friends with rude ungentle words
They scoff and bid me fly to thee!
O give me shelter in thy breast!
 O shield and shelter me!

' My Henry, I have given thee much,
I gave what I can ne'er recall,
I gave my heart, I gave my peace,
 O Heaven! I gave thee all.'

The Knight made answer to the Maid,
While to his heart he held her hand,
' Nine castles hath my noble sire,
     None statelier in the land.

' The fairest one shall be my love's,
The fairest castle of the nine!
Wait only till the stars peep out,
     The fairest shall be thine:

' Wait only till the hand of eve
Hath wholly closed yon western bars,
And through the dark we two will steal
     Beneath the twinkling stars! '—

' The dark? the dark? No! not the dark?
The twinkling stars? How, Henry? How?
O God! 'twas in the eye of noon
     He pledged his sacred vow!

' And in the eye of noon my love
Shall lead me from my mother's door,
Sweet boys and girls all clothed in white
     Strewing flowers before:

' But first the nodding minstrels go
With music meet for lordly bowers,
The children next in snow-white vests,
     Strewing buds and flowers!

' And then my love and I shall pace,
My jet black hair in pearly braids,
Between our comely bachelors
     And blushing bridal maids.'

1798.

ALICE DU CLOS, OR THE FORKED
TONGUE.

A BALLAD.

" One word with two meanings is the traitor's shield and
shaft: and a slit tongue be his blazon! "—*Caucasian Proverb.*

" THE Sun is not yet risen,
But the dawn lies red on the dew:
Lord Julian has stolen from the hunters away,
Is seeking, Lady, for you.
Put on your dress of green,
    Your buskins and your quiver;
Lord Julian is a hasty man,
    Long waiting brook'd he never.
I dare not doubt him, that he means
    To wed you on a day,
Your lord and master for to be,
    And you his lady gay,
O Lady! throw your book aside!
I would not that my Lord should chide."

Thus spake Sir Hugh the vassal knight
    To Alice, child of old Du Clos,
As spotless fair, as airy light
    As that moon-shiny doe,
The gold star on its brow, her sire's ancestral crest!
For ere the lark had left his nest,

She in the garden bower below
Sate loosely wrapt in maiden white,
Her face half drooping from the sight,
    A snow-drop on a tuft of snow!

O close your eyes, and strive to see
The studious maid, with book on knee,—
    Ah! earliest-open'd flower;
While yet with keen unblunted light
The morning star shone opposite
    The lattice of her bower—
Alone of all the starry host,
    As if in prideful scorn
Of flight and fear he stay'd behind,
    To brave th' advancing morn.

O! Alice could read passing well,
    And she was conning then
Dan Ovid's mazy tale of loves,
    And gods, and beasts, and men.

The vassal's speech, his taunting vein,
It thrill'd like venom thro' her brain;
    Yet never from the book
She rais'd her head, nor did she deign
    The knight a single look.

" Off, traitor friend! how dar'st thou fix
    Thy wanton gaze on me?
And why, against my earnest suit,
    Does Julian send by thee?

" Go, tell thy Lord, that slow is sure:
    Fair speed his shafts to-day!
I follow here a stronger lure,
    And chase a gentler prey."

She said: and with a baleful smile
    The vassal knight reel'd off—
Like a huge billow from a bark
    Toil'd in the deep sea-trough,
That shouldering sideways in mid plunge,
    Is travers'd by a flash,
And staggering onward, leaves the ear
    With dull and distant crash.

And Alice sate with troubled mien
A moment; for the scoff was keen,
    And thro' her veins did shiver!
Then rose and donn'd her dress of green,
    Her buskins and her quiver.

There stands the flow'ring may-thorn tree!
From thro' the veiling mist you see
    The black and shadowy stem;—
Smit by the sun the mist in glee
Dissolves to lightsome jewelry—
    Each blossom hath its gem!

With tear-drop glittering to a smile,
The gay maid on the garden-stile
    Mimics the hunter's shout.
" Hip! Florian, hip! To horse, to horse!
    Go, bring the palfrey out.
" My Julian's out with all his clan
    And, bonny boy, you wis,
Lord Julian is a hasty man,
    Who comes late, comes amiss."

Now Florian was a stripling squire,
  A gallant boy of Spain,
That toss'd his head in joy and pride,
Behind his Lady fair to ride,
  But blush'd to hold her train.

The huntress is in her dress of green,—
And forth they go; she with her bow,
  Her buskins and her quiver!—
The squire—no younger e'er was seen—
With restless arm and laughing een,
  He makes his javelin quiver.

And had not Ellen stay'd the race,
And stopp'd to see, a moment's space,
  The whole great globe of light
Give the last parting kiss-like touch
To the eastern ridge, it lack'd not much,
  They had o'erta'en the knight.

It chanced that up the covert lane,
  Where Julian waiting stood,
A neighbour knight prick'd on to join
  The huntsmen in the wood.

And with him must Lord Julian go,
  Tho' with an anger'd mind:
Betroth'd not wedded to his bride,
In vain he sought, 'twixt shame and pride,
  Excuse to stay behind.

He bit his lip, he wrung his glove,
He look'd around, he look'd above,

But pretext none could find or frame.
Alas! alas! and well-a-day!
It grieves me sore to think, to say,
That names so seldom meet with Love,
   Yet Love wants courage without a name!

Straight from the forest's skirt the trees
   O'er-branching, made an aisle,
Where hermit old might pace and chaunt
   As in a minster's pile.

From underneath its leafy screen,
   And from the twilight shade,
You pass at once into a green,
   A green and lightsome glade.

And there Lord Julian sate on steed;
   Behind him, in a round,
Stood knight and squire, and menial train;
Against the leash the greyhounds strain;
   The horses paw'd the ground.

When up the alley green, Sir Hugh
   Spurr'd in upon the sward,
And mute, without a word, did he
   Fall in behind his lord.

Lord Julian turn'd his steed half round,—
   " What! doth not Alice deign
To accept your loving convoy, knight?
Or doth she fear our woodland sleight,
   And joins us on the plain? "

With stifled tones the knight replied,
And look'd askance on either side,—
   "Nay, let the hunt proceed!—
The Lady's message that I bear,
I guess would scantly please your ear,
   And less deserves your heed.

"You sent betimes. Not yet unbarr'd
   I found the middle door;—
Two stirrers only met my eyes,
   Fair Alice, and one more.

"I came unlook'd for: and, it seem'd,
   In an unwelcome hour;
And found the daughter of Du Clos
   Within the lattic'd bower.

"But hush! the rest may wait. If lost
   No great loss, I divine;
And idle words will better suit
   A fair maid's lips than mine."

"God's wrath! speak out, man," Julian cried,
   O'ermaster'd by the sudden smart;—
And feigning wrath, sharp, blunt, and rude,
The knight his subtle shift pursued.—
"Scowl not at me; command my skill,
To lure your hawk back, if you will,
   But not a woman's heart.

"'Go! (said she) tell him,—slow is sure;
   Fair speed his shafts to-day!
I follow here a stronger lure,
   And chase a gentler prey.'

" The game, pardie, was full in sight,
That then did, if I saw aright,
   The fair dame's eyes engage;
For turning, as I took my ways,
I saw them fix'd with steadfast gaze
   Full on her wanton page."

The last word of the traitor knight
   It had but entered Julian's ear,—
From two o'erarching oaks between,
With glist'ning helm-like cap is seen,
   Borne on in giddy cheer,

A youth, that ill his steed can guide;
Yet with reverted face doth ride,
   As answering to a voice,
That seems at once to laugh and chide—
" Not mine, dear mistress," still he cried,
   " 'Tis this mad filly's choice."

With sudden bound, beyond the boy,
See! see! that face of hope and joy,
   That regal front! those cheeks aglow!
Thou needed'st but the crescent sheen,
A quiver'd Dian to have been,
   Thou lovely child of old Du Clos!

Dark as a dream Lord Julian stood,
Swift as a dream, from forth the wood,
   Sprang on the plighted Maid!
With fatal aim, and frantic force,
The shaft was hurl'd!—a lifeless corse,
Fair Alice from her vaulting horse,
   Lies bleeding on the glade.

             ? 1825.

FIRE, FAMINE, AND SLAUGHTER.

A WAR ECLOGUE.

The Scene a desolated Tract in La Vendée. FAMINE *is discovered lying on the ground: to her enter* FIRE *and* SLAUGHTER.

Fam. SISTERS! sisters! who sent you here?
Slau. [*to Fire*]. I will whisper it in her ear.
Fire. No! no! no!
Spirits hear what spirits tell:
'Twill make an holiday in Hell.
     No! no! no!
Myself, I named him once below,
And all the souls, that damned be,
Leaped up at once in anarchy,
Clapped their hands and danced for glee.
They no longer heeded me;
But laughed to hear Hell's burning rafters
Unwillingly re-echo laughters!
     No! no! no!
Spirits hear what spirits tell:
'Twill make an holiday in Hell!
  Fam. Whisper it, sister! so and so!
In a dark hint, soft and slow.
  Slau. Letters four do form his name—
And who sent you?
  Both.   The same! the same!
  Slau. He came by stealth, and unlocked my den,
And I have drunk the blood since then
Of thrice three hundred thousand men.

Both. Who bade you do 't?
Slau.   The same! the same!
Letters four do form his name.
He let me loose, and cried Halloo!
To him alone the praise is due.

  Fam. Thanks, sister, thanks! the men have bled,
Their wives and their children faint for bread.
I stood in a swampy field of battle;
With bones and skulls I made a rattle,
To frighten the wolf and carrion-crow
And the homeless dog—but they would not go.
So off I flew: for how could I bear
To see them gorge their dainty fare?
I heard a groan and a peevish squall,
And through the chink of a cottage-wall—
Can you guess what I saw there?

  Both. Whisper it, sister! in our ear.

  Fam. A baby beat its dying mother:
I had starved the one and was starving the other!

  Both. Who bade you do 't?
Fam.   The same! the same!
Letters four do form his name.
He let me loose, and cried Halloo!
To him alone the praise is due.

  Fire. Sisters! I from Ireland came!
Hedge and corn-fields all on flame,
I triumph'd o'er the setting sun!
And all the while the work was done,
On as I strode with my huge strides,
I flung back my head and I held my sides,
It was so rare a piece of fun
To see the sweltered cattle run
With uncouth gallop through the night,
Scared by the red and noisy light!

By the light of his own blazing cot
Was many a naked Rebel shot:
The house-stream met the flame and hissed,
While crash! fell in the roof, I wist,
On some of those old bed-rid nurses,
That deal in discontent and curses.
   Both. Who bade you do 't?
   Fire.   The same! the same!
Letters four do form his name.
He let me loose, and cried Halloo!
To him alone the praise is due.
   All. He let us loose, and cried Halloo!
How shall we yield him honour due?
   Fam. Wisdom comes with lack of food.
I'll gnaw, I'll gnaw the multitude,
Till the cup of rage o'erbrim:
They shall seize him and his brood—
   Slau. They shall tear him limb from limb!
   Fire. O thankless beldames and untrue!
And is this all that you can do
For him, who did so much for you?
Ninety months he, by my troth!
Hath richly catered for you both;
And in an hour would you repay
An eight years' work?—Away! away!
I alone am faithful! I
Cling to him everlastingly.

1797.

THE SPELL.

FROM *REMORSE*.   [*Mus*

Alvar. With no irreverent voice or uncouth charm
I call up the Departed!
                    Soul of Alvar!
Hear our soft suit, and heed my milder spell:
So may the Gates of Paradise, unbarr'd,
Cease thy swift toils!   Since haply thou art one
Of that innumerable company
Who in broad circle, lovelier than the rainbow,
Girdle this round earth in a dizzy motion,
With noise too vast and constant to be heard:
Fitliest unheard?   For oh, ye numberless,
And rapid Travellers! what ear unstunn'd,
What sense unmadden'd, might bear up against
The rushing of your congregated wings?   [*Musi*
Even now your living wheel turns o'er my head!
                    [*Music expressive of the movemen*
                        and images that follow.
Ye, as ye pass, toss high the desert Sands,
That roar and whiten, like a burst of waters,
A sweet appearance, but a dread illusion
To the parch'd caravan that roams by night!
And ye upbuild on the becalmed waves
That whirling pillar, which from Earth to Heaven
Stands vast, and moves in blackness!   Ye too split
The ice mount! and with fragments many and huge

Tempest the new-thaw'd sea, whose sudden gulphs
Suck in, perchance, some Lapland wizard's skiff!
Then round and round the whirlpool's marge ye dance,
Till from the blue swoln Corse the Soul toils out,
And joins your mighty Army.

> [*Here behind the scenes a voice sings the*
> *three words, ' Hear, Sweet Spirit '*
> Soul of Alvar!

Hear the mild spell, and tempt no blacker Charm!
By sighs unquiet, and the sickly pang
Of a half-dead, yet still undying Hope,
Pass visible before our mortal sense!
So shall the Church's cleansing rites be thine,
Her knells and masses that redeem the Dead!

SONG

Behind the Scenes, accompanied by the same
Instrument as before.

Hear, sweet spirit, hear the spell,
Lest a blacker charm compel!
So shall the midnight breezes swell
With thy deep long-lingering knell.

And at evening evermore,
In a chapel on the shore,
Shall the Chaunters sad and saintly,
Yellow tapers burning faintly,
Doleful Masses chaunt for thee,
Miserere Domine !

Hark! the cadence dies away
  On the quiet moonlight sea:
The boatmen rest their oars and say,
   Miserere Domine!   [*A long pause.*

Ordonio. The innocent obey nor charm nor spell!
My brother is in heaven.

DOMESTIC PEACE.

[FROM *THE FALL OF ROBESPIERRE*, ACT I.]

TELL me, on what holy ground
May Domestic Peace be found?
Halcyon daughter of the skies,
Far on fearful wings she flies,
From the pomp of Sceptered State,
From the Rebel's noisy hate.
In a cottaged vale She dwells,
Listening to the Sabbath bells!
Still around her steps are seen
Spotless Honour's meeker mien,
Love, the sire of pleasing fears,
Sorrow smiling through her tears,
And conscious of the past employ
Memory, bosom-spring of joy.

1794.

ON OBSERVING A BLOSSOM ON THE FIRST
OF FEBRUARY 1796.

SWEET flower! that peeping from thy russet stem
Unfoldest timidly, (for in strange sort
This dark, frieze-coated, hoarse, teeth-chattering
    month
Hath borrow'd Zephyr's voice, and gazed upon thee
With blue voluptuous eye) alas, poor Flower!
These are but flatteries of the faithless year.
Perchance, escaped its unknown polar cave,
Even now the keen North-East is on its way.

AD VILMUM AXIOLOGUM.

[TO WILLIAM WORDSWORTH.]

THIS be the meed, that thy song creates a thousand-
    fold echo!
Sweet as the warble of woods, that awakes at the
    gale of the morning!
List! the Hearts of the Pure, like caves in the
    ancient mountains
Deep, deep *in* the Bosom, and *from* the Bosom re-
    sound it,
Each with a different tone, complete or in musical
    fragments—
All have welcomed thy Voice, and receive and retain
    and prolong it!

This is the word of the Lord! it is spoken and Beings
    Eternal
Live and are borne as an Infant, the Eternal begets
    the Immortal,
Love is the Spirit of Life, and Music the Life of the
    Spirit!

MS.   ? 1805.

HEXAMETERS.

WILLIAM, my teacher, my friend! dear William and
    dear Dorothea!
Smooth out the folds of my letter, and place it on
    desk or on table;
Place it on table or desk; and your right hands
    loosely half-closing,
Gently sustain them in air, and extending the digit
    didactic,
Rest it a moment on each of the forks of the five-
    forkéd left hand,
Twice on the breadth of the thumb, and once on the
    tip of each finger;
Read with a nod of the head in a humouring recita-
    tivo;
And, as I live, you will see my hexameters hopping
    before you.
This is a galloping measure; a hop, and a trot, and a
    gallop!

All my hexameters fly, like stags pursued by the
    stag-hounds,
Breathless and panting, and ready to drop, yet
    flying still onwards,
I would full fain pull in my hard-mouthed runaway
    hunter;
But our English Spondeans are clumsy yet impotent
    curb-reins;
And so to make him go slowly, no way left have I
    but to lame him.

William, my head and my heart! dear Poet that
     feelest and thinkest!

Dorothy, eager of soul, my most affectionate sister!

Many a mile, O! many a wearisome mile are ye distant,

Long, long comfortless roads, with no one eye that
     doth know us.

O! it is all too far to send you mockeries idle:

Yea, and I feel it not right! But O! my friends, my
     beloved!

Feverish and wakeful I lie,—I am weary of feeling
     and thinking.

Every thought is worn *down*, I am weary yet cannot
     be vacant.

.   .   .   .   .   .

. . . my eyes are a burthen,

Now unwillingly closed, now open and aching with
     darkness.

O! what a life is the eye! what a fine and inscrut‧
     able essence!

Him that is utterly blind, nor glimpses the fire that
     warms him;

Him that never beheld the swelling breast of his
     mother;

Him that ne'er smiled at the bosom as babe that
     smiles in its slumber;

Even to him it exists, it stirs and moves in its prison;

Lives with a separate life, and ' Is it the Spirit ? ' he
     murmurs:

Sure it has thoughts of its own, and to see is only its
     language.

.   .   .   .   .

William my head and my heart! dear William and
     dear Dorothea!

You have all in each other; but I am lonely, and
     want you!

TO A GENTLEMAN.

[WILLIAM WORDSWORTH.]

COMPOSED ON THE NIGHT AFTER HIS RECITATION OF A
POEM ON THE GROWTH OF AN INDIVIDUAL MIND.

FRIEND of the wise! and Teacher of the Good!
Into my heart have I received that Lay
More than historic, that prophetic Lay
Wherein (high theme by thee first sung aright)
Of the foundations and the building up
Of a Human Spirit thou hast dared to tell
What may be told, to the understanding mind
Revealable; and what within the mind
By vital breathings secret as the soul
Of vernal growth, oft quickens in the heart
Thoughts all too deep for words!—

                              Theme hard as high!
Of smiles spontaneous, and mysterious fears
(The first-born they of Reason and twin-birth),
Of tides obedient to external force,
And currents self-determined, as might seem,
Or by some inner Power; of moments awful,
Now in thy inner life, and now abroad,
When power streamed from thee, and thy soul recei
The light reflected, as a light bestowed—
Of fancies fair, and milder hours of youth
Hyblean murmurs of poetic thought

Industrious in its joy, in vales and glens
Native or outland, lakes and famous hills!
Or on the lonely high-road, when the stars
Were rising; or by secret mountain-streams,
The guides and the companions of thy way!

Of more than Fancy, of the Social Sense
Distending wide, and man beloved as man,
Where France in all her towns lay vibrating
Like some becalmed bark beneath the burst
Of Heaven's immediate thunder, when no cloud
Is visible, or shadow on the main.
For thou wert there, thine own brows garlanded,
Amid the tremor of a realm aglow,
Amid a mighty nation jubilant,
When from the general heart of human kind
Hope sprang forth like a full-born Deity!
——Of that dear Hope afflicted and struck down,
So summoned homeward, thenceforth calm and sure
From the dread watch-tower of man's absolute self,
With light unwaning on her eyes, to look
Far on—herself a glory to behold,
The Angel of the vision! Then (last strain)
Of Duty, chosen Laws controlling choice,
Action and joy!—An orphic song indeed,
A song divine of high and passionate thoughts
To their own music chaunted!

O great Bard!
Ere yet that last strain dying awed the air,
With steadfast eye I viewed thee in the choir
Of ever-enduring men. The truly great
Have all one age, and from one visible space
Shed influence! They, both in power and act,

Q 43

Are permanent, and Time is not with *them*,
Save as it worketh *for* them, they *in* it.
Nor less a sacred Roll, than those of old,
And to be placed, as they, with gradual fame
Among the archives of mankind, thy work
Makes audible a linked lay of Truth,
Of Truth profound a sweet continuous lay,
Not learnt, but native, her own natural notes!
[Dear shall it be to every human heart,*
To me how more than dearest! me, on whom
Comfort from thee, and utterance of thy love,
Came with such heights and depths of harmony,
Such sense of wings uplifting, that its might
Scattered and quell'd me, till my thoughts became
A bodily tumult; and thy faithful hopes,
Thy hopes of me, dear Friend, by me unfelt!
Were troublous to me, almost as a voice,
Familiar once, and more than musical;
As a dear woman's Voice to one cast forth,
A wanderer with a worn-out heart forlorn,
Mid strangers pining with untended wounds.
O, Friend, too well thou know'st, of what sad years
The long suppression had benumb'd my soul,]
That, as I listen'd with a heart forlorn,
The pulses of my being beat anew:
And even as life returns upon the drowned,
Life's joy rekindling roused a throng of pains—
Keen pangs of Love, awakening as a babe
Turbulent, with an outcry in the heart;
And fears self-willed, that shunned the eye of hope;

* These lines in brackets were in the first version of the poem, and were omitted, owing, it is supposed, to the temporary estrangement between Wordsworth and Coleridge. *We owe their restoration to Mr Dykes Campbell*, whose note on the poem ought to be read.

And hope that scarce would know itself from fear;
Sense of past youth, and manhood come in vain,
And genius given, and knowledge won in vain;
And all which I had culled in wood-walks wild,
And all which patient toil had reared, and all,
Commune with *thee* had opened out—but flowers
Strewed on my corse, and borne upon my bier,
In the same coffin, for the self-same grave!

That way no more! and ill beseems it me,
Who came a welcomer in herald's guise,
Singing of glory, and futurity,
To wander back on such unhealthful road,
Plucking the poisons of self-harm!   And ill
Such intertwine beseems triumphal wreaths
Strew'd before *thy* advancing!

                              Nor do thou,
Sage Bard! impair the memory of that hour
Of thy communion with my nobler mind
By pity or grief, already felt too long!
Nor let my words import more blame than needs.
The tumult rose and ceased: for Peace is nigh
Where wisdom's voice has found a listening heart.
Amid the howl of more than wintry storms,
The halcyon hears the voice of vernal hours
Already on the wing.

                         Eve following eve,
Dear tranquil time, when the sweet sense of Home
Is sweetest! moments for their own sake hailed
And more desired, more precious, for thy song,
In silence listening, like a devout child,
My soul lay passive, by thy various strain

Driven as in surges now beneath the stars,
With momentary stars of my own birth,
Fair constellated foam, still darting off
Into the darkness; now a tranquil sea,
Outspread and bright, yet swelling to the moon.

And when—O Friend! my comforter and guide!
Strong in thyself, and powerful to give strength!—
Thy long sustained Song finally closed,
And thy deep voice had ceased—yet thou thyself
Wert still before my eyes, and round us both
That happy vision of beloved faces—
Scarce conscious, and yet conscious of its close
I sate, my being blended in one thought
(Thought was it? or aspiration? or resolve?)
Absorbed, yet hanging still upon the sound—
And when I rose, I found myself in prayer.

                                January 1807.

THE BLOSSOMING OF THE SOLITARY
DATE-TREE.

A LAMENT.

I.

IMAGINATION; honourable aims;
Free commune with the choir that cannot die;
Science and song; delight in little things,
The buoyant child surviving in the man;
Fields, forests, ancient mountains, ocean, sky,
With all their voices—O dare I accuse
My earthly lot as guilty of my spleen,

Or call my destiny niggard! O no! no!
It is her largeness, and her overflow,
Which being incomplete, disquieteth me so!

II.

For never touch of gladness stirs my heart,
But tim'rously beginning to rejoice
Like a blind Arab, that from sleep doth start
In lonesome tent, I listen for *thy* voice.
Beloved! 'tis not thine; thou art not there!
Then melts the bubble into idle air,
And wishing without hope I restlessly despair.

III.

The mother with anticipated glee
Smiles o'er the child, that, standing by her chair
And flatt'ning its round cheek upon her knee,
Looks up, and doth its rosy lips prepare
To mock the coming sounds. At that sweet sight
She hears her own voice with a new delight;
And if the babe perchance should lisp the notes
    aright,

IV.

Then is she tenfold gladder than before!
But should disease or chance the darling take,
What then avail those songs, which sweet of yore
Were only sweet for their sweet echo's sake?
Dear maid! no prattler at a mother's knee
Was e'er so dearly prized as I prize *thee*:
Why was I made for Love and Love denied to me?
                       1805.

A TOMBLESS EPITAPH.

'Tis true, Idoloclastes Satyrane!
(So call him, for so mingling blame with praise
And smiles with anxious looks, his earliest friends,
Masking his birth-name, wont to character
His wild-wood fancy and impetuous zeal)
'Tis true that, passionate for ancient truths,
And honouring with religious love the Great
Of elder times, he hated to excess,
With an unquiet and intolerant scorn,
The hollow puppets of an hollow age,
Ever idolatrous, and changing ever
Its worthless idols! Learning, power, and time,
(Too much of all) thus wasting in vain war
Of fervid colloquy. Sickness, 'tis true,
Whole years of weary days, besieged him close,
Even to the gates and inlets of his life!
But it is true, no less, that strenuous, firm,
And with a natural gladness, he maintained
The citadel unconquered, and in joy
Was strong to follow the delightful Muse.
For not a hidden path, that to the shades
Of the beloved Parnassian forest leads,
Lurked undiscovered by him; not a rill
There issues from the fount of Hippocrene,
But he had traced it upward to its source,
Through open glade, dark glen, and secret dell,
Knew the gay wild flowers on its banks, and culled
Its med'cinable herbs. Yea, oft alone,
Piercing the long-neglected holy cave,
The haunt obscure of old Philosophy.

He bade with lifted torch its starry walls
Sparkle, as erst they sparkled to the flame
Of odorous lamps tended by Saint and Sage.
O framed for calmer times and nobler hearts!
O studious Poet, eloquent for truth!
Philosopher! contemning wealth and death,
Yet docile, childlike, full of Life and Love!
Here, rather than on monumental stone,
This record of thy worth thy Friend inscribes,
Thoughtful, with quiet tears upon his cheek.

? 1809.

THE PAINS OF SLEEP.

ERE on my bed my limbs I lay,
It hath not been my use to pray
With moving lips or bended knees;
But silently, by slow degrees,
My spirit I to Love compose,
In humble trust mine eye-lids close,
With reverential resignation,
No wish conceived, no thought exprest,
Only a *sense* of supplication;
A sense o'er all my soul imprest
That I am weak, yet not unblest,
Since in me, round me, every where
Eternal Strength and Wisdom are.

But yester-night I pray'd aloud
In anguish and in agony,
Up-starting from the fiendish crowd
Of shapes and thoughts that tortured me:
A lurid light, a trampling throng,
Sense of intolerable wrong,

And whom I scorned, those only strong!
Thirst of revenge, the powerless will
Still baffled, and yet burning still!
Desire with loathing strangely mixed
On wild or hateful objects fixed.
Fantastic passions! maddening brawl!
And shame and terror over all!
Deeds to be hid which were not hid,
Which all confused I could not know
Whether I suffered, or I did:
For all seem'd guilt, remorse or woe,
My own or others still the same
Life-stifling fear, soul-stifling shame!

So two nights passed: the night's dismay
Saddened and stunned the coming day.
Sleep, the wide blessing, seemed to me
Distemper's worst calamity.
The third night, when my own loud scream
Had waked me from the fiendish dream,
O'ercome with sufferings strange and wild,
I wept as I had been a child;
And having thus by tears subdued
My anguish to a milder mood,
Such punishments, I said, were due
To natures deepliest stained with sin:
For aye entempesting anew
The unfathomable hell within
The horror of their deeds to view,
To know and loathe, yet wish and do!
Such griefs with such men well agree,
But wherefore, wherefore fall on me?
To be beloved is all I need,
And whom I love, I love indeed.

                                        1803.

AN ODE TO THE RAIN.

COMPOSED BEFORE DAYLIGHT, ON THE MORNING
    APPOINTED FOR THE DEPARTURE OF A VERY
    WORTHY, BUT NOT VERY PLEASANT VISITOR,
    WHOM IT WAS FEARED THE RAIN MIGHT DETAIN.

I.

I KNOW it is dark; and though I have lain,
Awake, as I guess, an hour or twain,
I have not once open'd the lids of my eyes,
But I lie in the dark, as a blind man lies.
O Rain! that I lie listening to,
You're but a doleful sound at best:
I owe you little thanks, 'tis true,
For breaking thus my needful rest!
Yet if, as soon as it is light,
O Rain! you will but take your flight,
I'll neither rail, nor malice keep,
Though sick and sore for want of sleep.
But only now, for this one day,
Do go, dear Rain! do go away!

II.

O Rain! with your dull two-fold sound,
The clash hard by, and the murmur all round!
You know, if you know aught, that we,
Both night and day, but ill agree:

For days and months, and almost years,
Have limp'd on through this vale of tears,
Since body of mine, and rainy weather,
Have lived on easy terms together.
Yet if, as soon as it is light,
O Rain! you will but take your flight,
Though you should come again to-morrow,
And bring with you both pain and sorrow;
Though stomach should sicken and knees should swe
I'll nothing speak of you but well.
But only now for this one day,
Do go, dear Rain! do go away!

III.

Dear Rain! I ne'er refused to say
You're a good creature in your way;
Nay, I could write a book myself,
Would fit a parson's lower shelf,
Showing how very good you are.—
What then? sometimes it must be fair!
And if sometimes, why not to-day?
Do go, dear Rain! do go away!

IV.

Dear Rain! if I've been cold and shy,
Take no offence! I'll tell you why.
A dear old Friend e'en now is here,
And with him came my sister dear;
After long absence now first met,
Long months by pain and grief beset—
We three dear friends! in truth, we groan
Impatiently to be alone.

We three, you mark! and not one more!
The strong wish makes my spirit sore.
We have so much to talk about,
So many sad things to let out;
So many tears in our eye-corners,
Sitting like little Jacky Horners—
In short, as soon as it is day,
Do go, dear Rain! do go away.

v.

And this I'll swear to you, dear Rain!
Whenever you shall come again,
Be you as dull as e'er you could
(And by the bye 'tis understood,
You're not so pleasant as you're good),
Yet, knowing well your worth and place,
I'll welcome you with cheerful face;
And though you stay'd a week or more,
Were ten times duller than before;
Yet with kind heart, and right good will,
I'll sit and listen to you still;
Nor should you go away, dear Rain!
Uninvited to remain.
But only now, for this one day,
Do go, dear Rain! do go away.

1802.

LINES COMPOSED IN A CONCERT-
ROOM

O GIVE me, from this heartless scene released,
 To hear our old musician, blind and grey,
(Whom stretching from my nurse's arms I kissed,)
 His Scottish tunes and warlike marches play,
By moonshine, on the balmy summer-night,
 The while I dance amid the tedded hay
With merry maids, whose ringlets toss in light.

Or lies the purple evening on the bay
Of the calm glossy lake, O let me hide
 Unheard, unseen, behind the alder-trees,
For round their roots the fisher's boat is tied,
 On whose trim seat doth Edmund stretch at ease,
And while the lazy boat sways to and fro,
 Breathes in his flute sad airs, so wild and slow,
That his own cheek is wet with quiet tears.

But O, dear Anne! when midnight wind careers,
And the gust pelting on the out-house shed
 Makes the cock shrilly in the rain-storm crow,
 To hear thee sing some ballad full of woe,
Ballad of ship-wreck'd sailor floating dead,
 Whom his own true-love buried in the sands!
Thee, gentle woman, for thy voice re-measures
Whatever tones and melancholy pleasures
 The things of Nature utter; birds or trees,
Or moan of ocean-gale in weedy caves,
Or where the stiff grass mid the heath-plant waves,
 Murmur and music thin of sudden breeze.

1799.

INSCRIPTION FOR A FOUNTAIN
ON A HEATH.

THIS Sycamore, oft musical with bees,—
Such tents the Patriarchs loved! O long unharmed
May all its aged boughs o'er-canopy
The small round basin, which this jutting stone
Keeps pure from falling leaves! Long may the
     Spring,
Quietly as a sleeping infant's breath,
Send up cold waters to the traveller
With soft and even pulse! Nor ever cease
Yon tiny cone of sand its soundless dance,
Which at the bottom, like a Fairy's Page,
As merry and no taller, dances still,
Nor wrinkles the smooth surface of the Fount.
Here twilight is and coolness: here is moss,
A soft seat, and a deep and ample shade.
Thou may'st toil far and find no second tree.
Drink, Pilgrim, here! Here rest! and if thy heart
Be innocent, here too shalt thou refresh
Thy spirit, listening to some gentle sound,
Or passing gale or hum of murmuring bees!

                        1802.

A SUNSET.

UPON the mountain's edge with light touch resting,
There a brief while the globe of splendour sits
  And seems a creature of the earth, but soon,
    More changeful than the Moon,
To wane fantastic his great orb submits,
Or cone or mow of fire: till sinking slowly
Even to a star at length he lessens wholly.

Abrupt, as Spirits vanish, he is sunk!
A soul-like breeze possesses all the wood.
  The boughs, the sprays have stood
As motionless as stands the ancient trunk!
But every leaf through all the forest flutters,
And deep the cavern of the mountain matters.

MS.   1805.

A THOUGHT SUGGESTED BY A VIEW

OF SADDLEBACK IN CUMBERLAND.

ON stern Blencartha's perilous height
  The winds are tyrannous and strong;
And flashing forth unsteady light
From stern Blencartha's skiey height,
  As loud the torrents throng!
Beneath the moon, in gentle weather,
They bind the earth and sky together.
But oh! the sky and all its forms, how quiet!
The things that seek the earth, how full of noise and
    riot!   1806.

TO NATURE.

It may indeed be phantasy when I
Essay to draw from all created things
Deep, heartfelt, inward joy that closely clings;
And trace in leaves and flowers that round me lie
Lessons of love and earnest piety.
So let it be; and if the wide world rings
In mock of this belief, it brings
Nor fear, nor grief, nor vain perplexity.
So will I build my altar in the fields,
And the blue sky my fretted dome shall be,
And the sweet fragrance that the wild flower yields
Shall be the incense I will yield to Thee,
The only God! and thou shalt not despise
Even me, the priest of this poor sacrifice.

? 1820.

A STRANGER MINSTREL.

[WRITTEN TO MRS. ROBINSON, A FEW WEEKS BEFORE
HER DEATH.]

As late on Skiddaw's mount I lay supine,
Midway th' ascent, in that repose divine
When the soul centred in the heart's recess
Hath quaff'd its fill of Nature's loveliness,
Yet still beside the fountain's marge will stay
   And fain would thirst again, again to quaff;
Then when the tear, slow travelling on its way,
   Fills up the wrinkles of a silent laugh—
In that sweet mood of sad and humorous thought
A form within me rose, within me wrought
With such strong magic, that I cried aloud,

' Thou ancient Skiddaw by thy helm of cloud,
And by thy many-colour'd chasms deep,
And by their shadows that for ever sleep,
By yon small flaky mists that love to creep
Along the edges of those spots of light,
Those sunny islands on thy smooth green height,
   And by yon shepherds with their sheep,
   And dogs and boys, a gladsome crowd,
   That rush even now with clamour loud
   Sudden from forth thy topmost cloud,
   And by this laugh, and by this tear,
   I would, old Skiddaw, she were here!

A lady of sweet song is she,
Her soft blue eye was made for thee!
O ancient Skiddaw, by this tear,
I would, I would that she were here!'

Then ancient Skiddaw, stern and proud,
    In sullen majesty replying,
Thus spake from out his helm of cloud
    (His voice was like an echo dying!):—
' She dwells belike in scenes more fair,
And scorns a mount so bleak and bare.'

I only sigh'd when this I heard,
Such mournful thoughts within me stirr'd
That all my heart was faint and weak,
    So sorely was I troubled!
No laughter wrinkled on my cheek,
    But O the tears were doubled!
But ancient Skiddaw green and high
Heard and understood my sigh;
And now, in tones less stern and rude,
As if he wish'd to end the feud,
Spake he, the proud response renewing
(His voice was like a monarch wooing):—

' Nay, but thou dost not know her might,
    The pinions of her soul how strong!
But many a stranger in my height
    Hath sung to me her magic song,
        Sending forth his ecstasy
        In her divinest melody,
    And hence I know her soul is free,
    She is where'er she wills to be,
    Unfetter'd by mortality!

R 43

Now to the " haunted beach " can fly,
    Beside the threshold scourged with waves,
    Now where the maniac wildly raves,
" *Pale moon, thou spectre of the sky !* "
    No wind that hurries o'er my height
Can travel with so swift a flight.
        I too, methinks, might merit
        The presence of her spirit!
        To me too might belong
The honour of her song and witching melody,
        Which most resembles me,
        Soft, various, and sublime,
        Exempt from wrongs of Time!'

Thus spake this mighty Mount, and I
Made answer, with a deep-drawn sigh:—
' Thou ancient Skiddaw, by this tear,
I would, I would that she were here!'

                                November 1800.

PORTRAIT OF SIR GEORGE BEAUMONT.

FROM THE APPENDIX TO *REMORSE.*

Zulimez (speaking of Alvar in the third person).

        SUCH was the noble Spaniard's own relation.
He told me, too, how in his early youth,
And his first travels, 'twas his choice or chance
To make long sojourn in sea-wedded Venice;
There won the love of that divine old man,
Courted by mightiest kings, the famous Titian!

Who, like a second and more lovely Nature,
By the sweet mystery of lines and colours
Changed the blank canvas to a magic mirror,
That made the Absent present; and to Shadows
Gave light, depth, substance, bloom, yea, thought
      and motion.
He loved the old man, and revered his art:
And though of noblest birth and ample fortune,
The young enthusiast thought it no scorn
But this inalienable ornament,
To be his pupil, and with filial zeal
By practice to appropriate the sage lessons,
Which the gay, smiling old man gladly gave.
The Art, he honoured thus, requited him:
And in the following and calamitous years
Beguiled the hours of his captivity.
    Alhadra. And then he framed this picture? and
      unaided
By arts unlawful, spell, or talisman!
    Alvar. A potent spell, a mighty talisman!
The imperishable memory of the deed,
Sustained by love, and grief, and indignation!
So vivid were the forms within his brain,
His very eyes, when shut, made pictures of them! *

                  ?1814.

---

  * " This passage is no mere fancy portrait, but a slight, yet not unfaithful profile of one who still lives, *nobilitate felix, arte clarior, vitâ colendissimus.*"

TO A YOUNG LADY.

[MISS LAVINIA POOLE.]

ON HER RECOVERY FROM A FEVER.

WHY need I say, Louisa dear!
How glad I am to see you here,
    A lovely convalescent;
Risen from the bed of pain and fear,
    And feverish heat incessant.

The sunny showers, the dappled sky,
The little birds that warble high,
    Their vernal loves commencing,
Will better welcome you than I
    With their sweet influencing.

Believe me, while in bed you lay,
Your danger taught us all to pray:
    You made us grow devouter!
Each eye looked up and seemed to say,
    How can we do without her?

Besides, what vexed us worse, we knew
They have no need of such as you
    In the place where you were going:
This World has angels all too few,
    And Heaven is overflowing!

March 31, 1798.

LINES TO W. LINLEY, ESQ.

WHILE HE SANG A SONG TO PURCELL'S MUSIC.

WHILE my young cheek retains its healthful hues,
   And I have many friends who hold me dear,
   Linley! methinks, I would not often hear
Such melodies as thine, lest I should lose
All memory of the wrongs and sore distress
   For which my miserable brethren weep!
   But should uncomforted misfortunes steep
My daily bread in tears and bitterness;
And if at death's dread moment I should lie
   With no beloved face at my bed-side,
To fix the last glance of my closing eye,
   Methinks such strains, breathed by my angel-guide,
Would make me pass the cup of anguish by,
   Mix with the blest, nor know that I had died!

1800.

LINES

WRITTEN IN COMMONPLACE BOOK OF MISS BARBOUR,
    DAUGHTER OF THE MINISTER OF THE U.S.A. TO
    ENGLAND.

CHILD of my muse! in Barbour's gentle hand
Go cross the main: thou seek'st no foreign land:
'Tis not the clod beneath our feet we name
Our country. Each heaven-sanctioned tie the same,
Laws, manners, language, faith, ancestral blood,
Domestic honour, awe of womanhood:—
With kindling pride thou wilt rejoice to see
Britain with elbow-room and doubly free!
Go seek thy countrymen! and if one scar
Still linger of that fratricidal war,
Look to the maid who brings thee from afar;
Be thou the olive-leaf and she the dove,
And say I greet thee with a brother's love!

                      S. T. COLERIDGE,
              GROVE, HIGHGATE, *August* 1829.

A CHRISTMAS CAROL.

I.

THE shepherds went their hasty way,
　　And found the lowly stable-shed
Where the Virgin-Mother lay:
　　And now they checked their eager tread,
For to the Babe, that at her bosom clung,
A Mother's song the Virgin-Mother sung.

II.

They told her how a glorious light,
　　Streaming from a heavenly throng,
Around them shone, suspending night!
　　While sweeter than a mother's song,
Blest Angels heralded the Saviour's birth,
Glory to God on high! and Peace on Earth.

III.

She listened to the tale divine,
　　And closer still the Babe she pressed;
And while she cried, the Babe is mine!
　　The milk rushed faster to her breast:
Joy rose within her, like a summer's morn;
Peace, Peace on Earth! the Prince of Peace is born.

TRANSLATION OF A PASSAGE IN OTTFRIED'S METRICAL PARAPHRASE OF THE GOSPEL.

She gave with joy her virgin breast;
She hid it not, she bared the breast
Which suckled that divinest babe!
Blessed, blessed were the breasts
Which the Saviour infant kiss'd;
And blessed, blessed was the mother
Who wrapp'd his limbs in swaddling clothes,
Singing placed him on her lap,
Hung o'er him with her looks of love,
And soothed him with a lulling motion.
Blessed; for she shelter'd him
From the damp and chilling air;
Blessed, blessed! for she lay
With such a babe in one blest bed,
Close as babes and mothers lie!
Blessed, blessed evermore,
With her virgin lips she kiss'd,
With her arms, and to her breast,
She embraced the babe divine,
Her babe divine the virgin mother!
There lives not on this ring of earth
A mortal that can sing her praise.
Mighty mother, virgin pure,
In the darkness and the night
For us she *bore* the heavenly Lord!

?1799.

SOMETHING CHILDISH, BUT VERY NATURAL.

WRITTEN IN GERMANY.

If I had but two little wings
   And were a little feathery bird,
      To you I'd fly, my dear!
But thoughts like these are idle things,
      And I stay here.

But in my sleep to you I fly:
   I'm always with you in my sleep!
      The world is all one's own,
But then one wakes, and where am I?
      All, all alone.

Sleep stays not, though a monarch bids:
   So I love to wake ere break of day:
      For though my sleep be gone,
Yet while 'tis dark, one shuts one's lids,
      And still dreams on.   *April* 23, 1799.

ANSWER TO A CHILD'S QUESTION.

Do you ask what the birds say? The Sparrow, the Dove,
The Linnet and Thrush say, ' I love and I love! '
In the winter they're silent—the wind is so strong;
What it says, I don't know, but it sings a loud song.
But green leaves, and blossoms, and sunny warm
      weather,
And singing, and loving—all come back together.
But the Lark is so brimful of gladness and love,
The green fields below him, the blue sky above,
That he sings, and he sings; and for ever sings he—
' I love my Love, and my Love loves me! '

                                          1802.

WHAT IS LIFE?

RESEMBLES life what once was deem'd of light,
Too ample in itself for human sight?
An absolute self—an element ungrounded—
All that we see, all colours of all shade
    By encroach of darkness made?—
Is very life by consciousness unbounded?
And all the thoughts, pains, joys of mortal breath,
A war-embrace of wrestling life and death?

                          1805.

PHANTOM.

ALL look and likeness caught from earth,
All accident of kin and birth,
Had pass'd away.   There was no trace
Of aught on that illumined face,
Upraised beneath the rifted stone
But of one spirit all her own;—
She, she herself, and only she,
Shone through her body visibly.

                          1804.

PHANTOM OR FACT.

A DIALOGUE IN VERSE.

AUTHOR.

A LOVELY form there sate beside my bed,
And such a feeding calm its presence shed,
A tender love so pure from earthly leaven,
That I unnethe the fancy might control,
'Twas my own spirit newly come from heaven,
Wooing its gentle way into my soul!
But ah! the change—It had not stirr'd, and yet—
Alas! that change how fain would I forget!
That shrinking back, like one that had mistook!
That weary, wandering, disavowing look!
'Twas all another, feature, look, and frame,
And still, methought, I knew, it was the same!

FRIEND.

This riddling tale, to what does it belong?
Is't history? vision? or an idle song?
Or rather say at once, within what space
Of time this wild disastrous change took place?

AUTHOR.

Call it a *moment's* work (and such it seems)
This tale's a fragment from the life of dreams;
But say, that years matur'd the silent strife,
And 'tis a record from the dream of life.

?1830.

LOVE'S APPARITION AND EVANISHMENT.

AN ALLEGORIC ROMANCE.

LIKE a lone Arab, old and blind,
Some caravan had left behind,
Who sits beside a ruin'd well,
Where the shy sand-asps bask and swell;
And now he hangs his aged head aslant,
And listens for a human sound—in vain!
And now the aid, which Heaven alone can grant,
Upturns his eyeless face from Heaven to gain;—
Even thus, in vacant mood, one sultry hour,
Resting my eye upon a drooping plant,
With brow low-bent, within my garden-bower,
I sate upon the couch of camomile;
And—whether 'twas as transient sleep, perchance,
Flitted across the idle brain, the while
I watch'd the sickly calm with aimless scope,
In my own heart; or that, indeed a trance,
Turn'd my eye inward—thee, O genial Hope,
Love's elder sister! thee did I behold,
Drest as a bridesmaid, but all pale and cold,
With roseless cheek, all pale and cold and dim,
    Lie lifeless at my feet!
And then came Love, a sylph in bridal trim,
    And stood beside my seat;
She bent, and kiss'd her sister's lips,
    As she was wont to do;—

Alas! 'twas but a chilling breath
Woke just enough of life in death
  To make Hope die anew.

L'ENVOY.

In vain we supplicate the Powers above;
There is no resurrection for the Love
That, nursed in tenderest care, yet fades away
In the chill'd heart by gradual self-decay.

1833.

DUTY SURVIVING SELF-LOVE.

THE ONLY SURE FRIEND OF DECLINING LIFE.

A SOLILOQUY.

UNCHANGED within, to see all changed without,
Is a blank lot and hard to bear, no doubt.
Yet why at others' wanings should'st thou fret?
Then only might'st thou feel a just regret,
Hadst thou withheld thy love or hid thy light
In selfish forethought of neglect and slight.
O wiselier then, from feeble yearnings freed,
While, and *on whom*, thou may'st—shine on! nor heed
Whether the object by reflected light
Return thy radiance or absorb it quite:
And though thou notest from thy safe recess
Old friends burn dim, like lamps in noisome air,
Love them for what they *are*; nor love them less,
Because to *thee* they are not what they *were*.

1826.

WORK WITHOUT HOPE.

LINES COMPOSED 21ST FEBRUARY 1827.

ALL Nature seems at work. Slugs leave their lair—
The bees are stirring—birds are on the wing—
And Winter slumbering in the open air,
Wears on his smiling face a dream of Spring!
And I the while, the sole unbusy thing,
Nor honey make, nor pair, nor build, nor sing.

Yet well I ken the banks where amaranths blow,
Have traced the fount whence streams of nectar flo
Bloom, O ye amaranths! bloom for whom ye may,
For me ye bloom not! Glide, rich streams, away!
With lips unbrightened, wreathless brow, I stroll:
And would you learn the spells that drowse my sou.
Work without Hope draws nectar in a sieve,
And Hope without an object cannot live.

1827.

LOVE, HOPE, AND PATIENCE IN EDUCATION.

O'ER wayward childhood would'st thou hold firm rule,
And sun thee in the light of happy faces;
Love, Hope, and Patience, these must be thy graces,
And in thine own heart let them first keep school.
For as old Atlas on his broad neck places
Heaven's starry globe, and there sustains it;—so
Do these upbear the little world below
Of Education,—Patience, Love, and Hope.
Methinks, I see them group'd in seemly show,
The straiten'd arms upraised, the palms aslope,
And robes that touching as adown they flow,
Distinctly blend, like snow emboss'd in snow.

O part them never!   If Hope prostrate lie,
             Love too will sink and die.
But Love is subtle, and doth proof derive
From her own life that Hope is yet alive;
And bending o'er, with soul-transfusing eyes,
And the soft murmurs of the mother dove,
Wooes back the fleeting spirit, and half supplies;—
Thus Love repays to Hope what Hope first gave to
        Love.
Yet haply there will come a weary day,
             When overtask'd at length
Both Love and Hope beneath the load give way.
Then with a statue's smile, a statue's strength,
Stands the mute sister, Patience, nothing loth,
And both supporting does the work of both.

                                    1829.

SELF-KNOWLEDGE.

Γνῶθι σεαυτόν!—and is this the prime
And heaven-sprung adage of the olden time!—
Say, canst thou make thyself?—Learn first that
    trade;—
Haply thou mayst know what thyself had made.
What hast thou, Man, that thou dar'st call thine
    own?—
What is there in thee, Man, that can be known?—
Dark fluxion, all unfixable by thought,
A phantom dim of past and future wrought,
Vain sister of the worm,—life, death, soul, clod—
Ignore thyself, and strive to know thy God!

1832.

EPITAPH.

Stop, Christian passer-by!—Stop, child of God,
And read with gentle breast.   Beneath this sod
A poet lies, or that which once seem'd he.—
O, lift one thought in prayer for S. T. C.;
That he who many a year with toil of breath
Found death in life, may here find life in death!
Mercy for praise—to be forgiven for fame
He ask'd, and hoped, through Christ.
        Do thou the same!

9th November 1833.

NOTES.

1. *Æolian Harp*, p. 67. Coleridge, *in* 1797, thought this poem the most perfect he had ever written. It belongs to the early time.

2. *A quiet place*, p. 69. The title in the Poems is " Reflections on having left a Place of Retirement." I have left out the reflections, and therefore changed the title.

3. *Fears in Solitude*, p. 80. A great part of this poem, excessively like a poor sermon, is omitted.

4. *The Nightingale*, p. 83. The friend and our sister were William and Dorothy Wordsworth; and the ' gentle maid ' is also Dorothy.

5. *Ode to the Departing Year*, p. 95. This Ode was written on the 24th, 25th, and 26th days of December 1796, and published separately on the last day of the year.

6. *France : an Ode*, p. 101. The following Argument, which Coleridge placed before the Ode, condenses his position towards the French Revolution :—

" ARGUMENT.

" *First Stanza.* An invocation to those objects in Nature, the contemplation of which had inspired the Poet with a devotional love of Liberty. *Second Stanza.* The exultation of the Poet at the commencement of the French Revolution, and his unqualified abhorrence of the Alliance against the Republic. *Third Stanza.* The blasphemies and horrors during the domination of the Terrorists regarded by the Poet as a transient storm, and as the natural consequence of the former despotism and of the foul superstition of Popery. Reason, indeed, began to suggest many apprehensions ; yet still the Poet struggled to retain the hope that France would make conquests by no other means than by presenting to the observation of Europe a people more happy and better instructed than under other forms of Government. *Fourth Stanza.* Switzerland, and the Poet's recantation. *Fifth Stanza.* An Address to Liberty, in which the Poet expresses his conviction that those feelings and that grand *ideal* of Freedom which the mind attains by its contemplation of its individual nature, and of the sublime surrounding objects (see stanza the first), do not belong to men as a society, nor can possibly be either gratified or realised under any form of human government, but belong to the individual man, so far as he is pure, and inflamed with the love and adoration of God in Nature."

7. *Dejection : an Ode*, p. 105. The poem was originally addressed to Wordsworth, then to Wordsworth under the name of Edmund. In 1817, ' Lady ' took the place of Edmund. ' Otway ' is used instead of Edmund, and it is plain that the lines 117-125 refer to the poem of *Lucy Gray*, which was printed in 1800.

8. *Hymn to the Earth*, p. 111. This is a translation, and partly an expansion, of the opening of F. L. Stolberg's *Hymne an die Erde ;* and *On a Cataract*, which follows, is also improved from Stolberg's lines on this subject. The originals of these, and of Schiller's *Visit of the Gods*, will be found in the Notes of Mr Dykes Campbell's Edition of Coleridge's Poems.

9. *Hymn before Sunrise*, p. 116. Coleridge was never at Chamouni, and he was indebted for the germ of the poem, and for many of its words and images, to the stanzas, *Chamouni at Sunrise*, written by Frederike Brun, and addressed to Klopstock. The original stanzas are inserted in Dykes Campbell's Notes.

10. *The Ancient Mariner*, p. 121. In one of the Appendices annexed to Mr Dykes Campbell's Edition of the Poems, the original form of the *Ancient Mariner*, as published in the *Lyrical Ballads*, will be found ; and it is well worth while to inwardly digest the remarkable changes which Coleridge made in his poem. Wordsworth thus described the origin of the poem to Miss Fenwick:—

" In the autumn of 1797 [really November], he [Coleridge], my sister, and myself, started from Alfoxden pretty late in the afternoon with a view to visit Linton and the Valley of Stones, near to it. Accordingly we set off, and proceeded along the Quantock Hills towards Watchet, and in the course of this walk was planned the poem of *The Ancient Mariner*, founded on a dream, as Mr Coleridge said, of his friend Mr Cruikshank. Much the greatest part of the story was Mr Coleridge's invention ; but certain parts I suggested : for example, some crime was to be committed which should bring upon the Old Navigator, as Coleridge afterwards delighted to call him, the spectral persecution, as a consequence of that crime and his own wanderings. I had been reading in Shelvocke's *Voyages*, a day or two before, that, while doubling Cape Horn, they frequently saw albatrosses in that latitude, the largest sort of sea-fowl, some extending their wings twelve or thirteen feet. ' Suppose,' said I, ' you represent him as having killed one of these birds on entering the South Sea, and that the tutelary spirits of these regions take upon them to avenge the crime.' The incident was thought fit for the purpose, and adopted accordingly. I also suggested the navigation of the ship by the dead men, but do not recollect that I had anything more to do with the scheme of the poem. The gloss with which it was subsequently accompanied was not thought of by either of us at the time—at least not a hint of it was given to me, and I have no doubt it was a gratuitous afterthought. We began the composition together on that, to me, memorable evening. I furnished two or three lines at the beginning of the poem, in particular—

> ' And listened like a three years' child:
> The Mariner had his will.'

These trifling contributions, all but one, which Mr Coleridge has with unnecessary scrupulosity recorded, slipped out of his mind, as they well might. As we endeavoured to proceed conjointly (I speak of the same evening), our respective manners proved so widely different that it would have been quite presumptuous in me to do anything but separate from an undertaking upon which I could only have been a clog." —*Memoirs of William Wordsworth*, London, 1851, vol. i. pp. 107, 108.

A further reminiscence of Wordsworth was communicated by the Rev. Alex. Dyce to H. N. Coleridge:—

" When my truly-honoured friend Mr Wordsworth was last in London, soon after the appearance of De Quincey's papers in *Tait's Magazine*, he dined with me in Gray's Inn, and made the following statement, which, I am quite sure, I give you correctly: '*The Ancient Mariner* was founded on a strange dream which a friend of Coleridge had, who fancied he saw a skeleton ship with figures in it. We had both determined to write some poetry for a monthly magazine, the profits of which were to defray the expenses of a little excursion we were to make together. *The Ancient Mariner* was intended for this periodical, but was too long. I had very little share in the composition of it, for I soon found that the style of Coleridge and myself would not assimilate. Besides the lines (in the fourth part)—

> ' And thou art long, and lank, and brown,
> As is the ribbed sea-sand '—

I wrote the stanza (in the first part)—

> ' He holds him with his glittering eye—
> The Wedding-Guest stood still,
> And listens like a three-years' child:
> The Mariner hath his will '—

and four or five lines more in different parts of the poem, which I could not now point out. The idea of ' *shooting an albatross* ' *was mine ; for I had been reading Shelvocke's Voyages, which probably Coleridge never saw.* I also suggested the reanimation of the dead bodies to work the ship.' " —(Note in *Poems* of S.T.C. ed. 1852.)

The following is Coleridge's account of the matter, as given in Chap. XIV. of his *Biog. Lit.*:—

" During the first year that Mr Wordsworth and I were neighbours, our conversations turned frequently on the two cardinal points of poetry—the power of exciting the sympathy of the reader by a faithful adherence to the truth of nature, and the power of giving the interest of novelty by the modifying colours of imagination. The sudden charm which accidents of light and shade, which moonlight or sunset, diffused over a known and familiar landscape, appeared to represent the practicability of combining both. These are the poetry of nature. The thought suggested itself (to which of us I do not recollect), that a series of poems might be composed of two sorts. In the one, the incidents and agents were to be, in part at least, supernatural; and the excellence aimed at was to consist in the interesting of the affections by the dramatic truth of such emotions as would naturally accompany such situations, supposing them real. And real in this sense they have been to every human being who, from whatever source of delusion, has at any time believed himself under supernatural agency. For the second class, subjects were to be chosen from ordinary life; the characters and incidents were to be such as will be found in every village and its vicinity, where there is a meditative and feeling mind to seek after them, or to notice them when they present themselves.

" In this idea originated the plan of the *Lyrical Ballads*, in which it was agreed that my endeavours should be directed to persons and characters supernatural, or at least romantic; yet so as to transfer from our inward nature a human interest and a semblance of truth, sufficient to procure for these shadows of imagination that willing suspension of disbelief for the moment, which constitutes poetic faith. Mr Wordsworth, on the other hand, was to propose to himself as his object to give the charm of novelty to things of every day, and to excite a feeling analogous to the supernatural, by awakening the mind's attention from the lethargy of custom, and directing it to the loveliness and the wonders of the world before us; an inexhaustible treasure, but for which, in consequence of the film of familiarity and selfish solicitude, we have eyes, yet see not, ears that hear not, and hearts that neither feel nor understand.

" With this view I wrote *The Ancient Mariner*, and was preparing, among other poems, the *Dark Ladie*, and the *Christabel*, in which I should have more nearly realised my ideal than I had done in my first attempt. But Mr Wordsworth's industry had proved so much more successful, and the number of his poems so much greater, that my compositions, instead of forming a balance, appeared rather an interpolation of heterogeneous matter. Mr Wordsworth added two or three poems written in his own character, in the impassioned, lofty, and sustained diction which is characteristic of his genius. In this form the *Lyrical Ballads* were published."

As to its morality, Coleridge said in his *Table Talk* :—

" Mrs Barbauld once told me that she admired *The Ancient Mariner* very much, but that there were two faults in it,—it was improbable, and had no moral. As for the probability, I owned that that might admit some question; but as to the want of a moral, I told her that in my own judgment the poem had too much; and that the only, or chief fault, if I might say so, was the obtrusion of the moral sentiment so openly on the reader as a principle or cause of action in a work of such pure imagination. It ought to have had no more moral than the Arabian Nights' tale of the merchant's sitting down to eat dates by the side of a well, and throwing the shells aside, and lo! a genie starts up, and says he *must* kill the aforesaid merchant, *because* one of the date shells had, it seems, put out the eye of the genie's son."—*Table Talk*, May 31, 1830.

He expresses the same indignation as to the necessity of a moral with regard to *The Raven*, to which he added, after its first publication, the following lines at the close:—

> " We must not think so, but forget and forgive;
> And what Heaven gives life to, we'll let it live "—

Mr Campbell found, he says, " in the margin of a copy now in the possession of Mr Stuart (by whose courtesy I am enabled to print it), the following note of Coleridge ":—
" Added thro' cowardly fear of the Goody! What a Hollow

where the Heart of Faith ought to be, does it not betray—this alarm concerning Christian morality, that will not permit a Raven to be a Raven, nor a Fox a Fox, but demands conventicular justice to be inflicted on their un-Christian conduct, or at least an antidote to be annexed."

11. *Encinctured with a twine of leaves*, p. 169.   Here is the prose of the *Wanderings of Cain*, only the introductory stanza of which exists in *Encinctured, etc.*

THE WANDERINGS OF CAIN.

CANTO II.

" A little further, O my father, yet a little further, and we shall come into the open moonlight." Their road was through a forest of fir-trees; at its entrance the trees stood at distances from each other, and the path was broad, and the moonlight and the moonlight shadows reposed upon it, and appeared quietly to inhabit that solitude.   But soon the path winded and became narrow; the sun at high noon sometimes speckled, but never illumined it, and now it was dark as a cavern.

" It is dark, O my father!" said Enos, " but the path under our feet is smooth and soft, and we shall soon come out into the open moonlight."

" Lead on, my child!" said Cain; " guide me, little child!" And the innocent little child clasped a finger of the hand which had murdered the righteous Abel, and he guided his father. " The fir branches drip upon thee, my son." " Yea, pleasantly, father, for I ran fast and eagerly to bring thee the pitcher and the cake, and my body is not yet cool. How happy the squirrels are that feed on these fir-trees! they leap from bough to bough, and the old squirrels play round their young ones in the nest.   I clomb a tree yesterday at noon, O my father, that I might play with them, but they leaped away from the branches, even to the slender twigs did they leap, and in a moment I beheld them on another tree. Why, O my father, would they not play with me?   I would be good to them, as thou art good to me: and I groaned to them, even as thou groanest when thou givest me to eat, and when thou coverest me at evening, and as often as I stand at thy knee and thine eyes look at me." Then Cain stopped, and stifling his groans, he sank to the earth, and the child Enos stood in the darkness beside him.

And Cain lifted up his voice and cried bitterly, and said, "The Mighty One that persecuteth me is on this side and on that; he pursueth my soul like the wind, like the sand-blast he passeth through me; he is around me even as the air! O that I might be utterly no more! I desire to die—yea, the things that never had life, neither move they upon the earth—behold! they seem precious to mine eyes. O that a man might live without the breath of his nostrils. So I might abide in darkness, and blackness, and an empty space! Yea, I would lie down, I would not rise, neither would I stir my limbs till I became as the rock in the den of the lion, on which the young lion resteth his head whilst he sleepeth. For the torrent that roareth far off hath a voice: and the clouds in heaven look terribly on me; the Mighty One who is against me speaketh in the wind of the cedar grove; and in silence am I dried up." Then Enos spake to his father, "Arise, my father, arise, we are but a little way from the place where I found the cake and the pitcher." And Cain said, "How knowest thou?" and the child answered—"Behold, the bare rocks are a few of thy strides distant from the forest; and while even now thou wert lifting up thy voice, I heard the echo." Then the child took hold of his father, as if he would raise him: and Cain being faint and feeble rose slowly on his knees and pressed himself against the trunk of a fir, and stood upright and followed the child.

The path was dark till within three strides' length of its termination, when it turned suddenly; the thick black trees formed a low arch, and the moonlight appeared for a moment like a dazzling portal. Enos ran before and stood in the open air; and when Cain, his father, emerged from the darkness, the child was affrighted. For the mighty limbs of Cain were wasted as by fire; his hair was as the matted curls on the bison's forehead, and so glared his fierce and sullen eye beneath: and the black abundant locks on either side, a rank and tangled mass, were stained and scorched, as though the grasp of a burning iron hand had striven to rend them; and his countenance told in a strange and terrible language of agonies that had been, and were, and were still to continue to be.

The scene around was desolate; as far as the eye could reach it was desolate: the bare rocks faced each other, and left a long and wide interval of thin white sand. You might wander on and look round and round, and peep into the crevices of the rocks and discover nothing that acknowledged the influence of the seasons. There was no spring, no summer, no autumn: and the winter's snow, that would have been lovely, fell not on these hot rocks and scorching sands. Never morning lark had poised himself over this desert; but the huge serpent often hissed there beneath the talons of the vulture, and the vulture screamed, his wings imprisoned within the coils of the serpent. The pointed and shattered summits of the ridges of the rocks made a rude mimicry of human concerns, and seemed to prophesy mutely of things that then were not—steeples, and battlements, and ships with naked masts. As far from the wood as a boy might sling a pebble of the brook, there was one rock by itself at a small distance from the main ridge. It had been precipitated there perhaps by the groan which the Earth uttered when our first father fell. Before you approached, it appeared to lie flat on the ground, but its base slanted from its point, and between its point and the sands a tall man might stand upright. It was here that Enos had found the pitcher and cake, and to this place he led his father. But ere they had reached the rock they beheld a human shape: his back was towards them, and they were advancing unperceived, when they heard him smite his breast and cry aloud, " Woe is me! woe is me! I must never die again, and yet I am perishing with thirst and hunger."

Pallid, as the reflection of the sheeted lightning on the heavy-sailing night cloud, became the face of Cain; but the child Enos took hold of the shaggy skin, his father's robe, and raised his eyes to his father, and listening whispered, " Ere yet I could speak, I am sure, O my father, that I heard that voice. Have not I often said that I remembered a sweet voice? O my father! this is it: " and Cain trembled exceedingly. The voice was sweet indeed, but it was thin and querulous, like that of a feeble slave in misery, who despairs altogether, yet cannot refrain himself from weeping and lamentation. And, behold! Enos glided forward, and creeping softly round the base of the rock, stood before the stranger, and looked up into his face. And the Shape shrieked, and turned round, and Cain beheld him, that his limbs and his face were those of his brother Abel whom he had killed! And Cain stood like one who struggles in his sleep because of the exceeding terribleness of a dream.

Thus as he stood in silence and darkness of soul, the Shape fell at his feet, and embraced his knees, and cried out with a bitter outcry, " Thou eldest born of Adam, whom Eve, my mother, brought forth, cease to torment me! I was feeding my flocks in green pastures by the side of quiet rivers, and thou killedst me; and now I am in misery." Then Cain closed his eyes, and hid them with his hands; and again he opened his eyes, and looked around him, and said to Enos, "What beheldest thou? Didst thou hear a voice, my son?" "Yes, my father, I beheld a man in unclean garments, and he uttered a sweet voice, full of lamentation." Then Cain raised up the Shape that was like Abel, and said:—" The Creator of our father, who had respect unto thee, and unto thy offering, wherefore hath he forsaken thee?" Then the shape shrieked a second time, and rent his garment, and his naked skin was like the white sands beneath their feet; and he shrieked yet a third time, and threw himself on his face upon the sand that was black with the shadow of the rock, and Cain and Enos sate beside him; the child by his right hand, and Cain by his left. They were all three under the rock, and within the shadow. The Shape that was like Abel raised himself up, and spake to the child, " I know where the cold waters are, but I may not drink, wherefore didst thou then take away my pitcher?" But Cain said, " Didst thou not find favour in the sight of the Lord thy God?" The Shape answered, " The Lord is God of the living only, the dead have another God." Then the child Enos lifted up his eyes and prayed; but Cain rejoiced secretly in his heart. "Wretched shall they be all the days of their mortal life," exclaimed the Shape, " who sacrifice worthy and acceptable sacrifices to the God of the dead; but after death their toil ceaseth. Woe is me, for I was well beloved by the God of the living, and cruel wert thou, O my brother, who didst snatch me away from his power and his dominion." Having uttered these words, he rose suddenly, and fled over the sands: and Cain said in his heart, " The curse of the Lord is on me; but who is the God of the dead?" and he ran after the Shape, and the Shape fled shrieking over the sands, and the sand rose like white mists behind the steps of Cain, but the feet of him that was like Abel disturbed not the sands. He greatly outrun Cain, and turning short, he wheeled round, and came again to the rock where they had been sitting, and where Enos still stood; and the child caught hold of his garment as he passed by, and he fell upon the ground. And Cain stopped, and beholding him not, said, " He has passed into the dark woods," and he walked slowly back to the rocks; and when he reached it the child told him that he had caught hold of his garment as he passed by, and that the man had fallen upon the ground; and Cain once more sate beside him, and said, " Abel, my brother, I would lament for thee, but that the spirit within me is withered, and burnt up with extreme agony. Now, I pray thee, by thy flocks, and by thy pastures, and by the quiet rivers which thou lovedst, that thou tell me all that thou knowest. Who is the God of the dead? where doth he make his dwelling? what sacrifices are acceptable unto him? for I have offered, but have not been received; I have prayed, and have not been heard; and how can I be afflicted more than I already am?" The Shape arose and answered, "O that thou hadst had pity on me as I will have pity on thee. Follow me, Son of Adam! and bring thy child with thee!"

And they three passed over the white sands between the rocks, silent as the shadows.   1798.

12. *Kubla Khan*, p. 170. I give Coleridge's note—

OF THE FRAGMENT OF KUBLA KHAN.

The following fragment is here published at the request of a poet of great and deserved celebrity [presumably Byron], and, as far as the Author's own opinions are concerned, rather as a psychological curiosity, than on the ground of any supposed *poetic* merits.

In the summer of the year 1797, the Author, then in ill health, had retired to a lonely farm-house between Porlock and Linton, on the Exmoor confines of Somerset and Devonshire. In consequence of a slight indisposition, an anodyne had been prescribed, from the effects of which he fell asleep in his chair at the moment that he was reading the following sentence, or words of the same substance, in "Purchas's Pilgrimage": "Here the Khan Kubla commanded a palace to be built, and a stately garden thereunto. And thus ten miles of fertile ground were inclosed with a wall." [1] The Author continued for about three hours in a profound sleep, at least of the external senses, during which time he has the most vivid confidence that he could not have composed less than from two to three hundred lines; if that indeed can be called composition in which all the images rose up before him as *things*, with a parallel production of the correspondent expressions, without any sensation or consciousness of effort. On awaking he appeared to himself to have a distinct recollection of the whole, and taking his pen, ink, and paper, instantly and eagerly wrote down the lines that are here preserved. At this moment he was unfortunately called out by a person on business from Porlock, and detained by him

[1] "In Xamdu did Cublai Can build a stately Palace, encompassing sixteene miles of plaine ground with a wall, wherein are fertile Meddowes, pleasant Springs, delightfull Streames, and all sorts of beasts of chase and game, and in the middest thereof a sumptuous house of pleasure."— PURCHAS *his Pilgrimage*; *Lond. fol.* 1626, Bk. iv. chap. xiii. p. 418.— ED.

bove an hour, and on his return to his room, found, to his
o small surprise and mortification, that though he still re-
ained some vague and dim recollection of the general pur-
ort of the vision, yet, with the exception of some eight or ten
cattered lines and images, all the rest had passed away like
he images on the surface of a stream into which a stone has
een cast, but, alas! without the after-restoration of the
atter!

> " Then all the charm
> Is broken—all that phantom-world so fair
> Vanishes, and a thousand circlets spread,
> And each mis-shape the other.   Stay awhile,
> Poor youth! who scarcely dar'st lift up thine eyes—
> The stream will soon renew its smoothness, soon
> The visions will return!   And lo, he stays,
> And soon the fragments dim of lovely forms
> Come trembling back, unite, and now once more
> The pool becomes a mirror."
> (From *The Picture ; or, the Lover's Resolution*.)

Yet from the still-surviving recollections in his mind, the
Author has frequently purposed to finish for himself what
had been originally, as it were, given to him.   Σάρμον ἄδιον
ἴσω: but the to-morrow is yet to come.

13. *Fable is Love's world*, p. 172.   From *The Piccolomini*,
Act II. Scene iv.

14. *Fancy in Nubibus*, p. 175.   The last five lines are
imitated from Stolberg's *An das Meer*.

15. *Catullian Hendecasyllables*, p. 176.   This is a free translation from Matthisson's Milesisches Mährchen.   See, for
original, Mr Campbell's Edition of the Poems of Coleridge.

16. *The Snow Drop*, p. 190.   I have omitted one stanza.

17. *The Spell*, p. 236.   From *Remorse*, Act III. Scene i.

18. *On observing a blossom*, p. 239.   Some lines are here, at
the close, omitted.

19. *A tombless Epitaph*, p. 248.   Satyrane is Coleridge
himself.

20. *Lines composed in a Concert Room*, p. 254.   This is only
the close of the poem.   It can well stand alone.   The
previous verses are not good.

21. *A Christmas Carol*, p. 265.   I have only printed the
first 3 verses.

INDEX TO FIRST LINES

287

...ch of the thirteen classifications in this list (except BIOGRAPHY)
... olumes are arranged alphabetically under the *authors' names*.
...nthologies and works by various hands are listed under titles.
...re authors appear in more than one section, a cross-reference
...ven, viz.: (*See also* FICTION). The number at the end of each
...is the number of the volume in the series.

BIOGRAPHY

BIOGRAPHY—continued

CLASSICAL

ESSAYS AND BELLES-LETTRES

ESSAYS AND BELLES-LETTRES—*continue.*

FICTION

FICTION—*continued*

FICTION—continued

FICTION—*continued*

FICTION—continued

HISTORY

HISTORY—continued

ORATORY

PHILOSOPHY AND THEOLOGY

POETRY AND DRAMA

POETRY AND DRAMA—continued

REFERENCE

ROMANCE

SCIENCE

TRAVEL AND TOPOGRAPHY

FOR YOUNG PEOPLE

FOR YOUNG PEOPLE—*continued*

Made in Great Britain at The Temple Press, Letchworth, Herts (W 127)